Airs & Dances

A Collection of Scottish Strathspeys for violin and other melody instruments

Compiled by Mara Shea

Accompanying chords by Julie Gorka

Illustrations by Lisa McDonald

Online Audio www.melbay.com/22123EB

1 2 3 4 5 6 7 8 9 0

Visit us on the Web at www.melbay.com — E-mail us at email@melbay.com

Contents

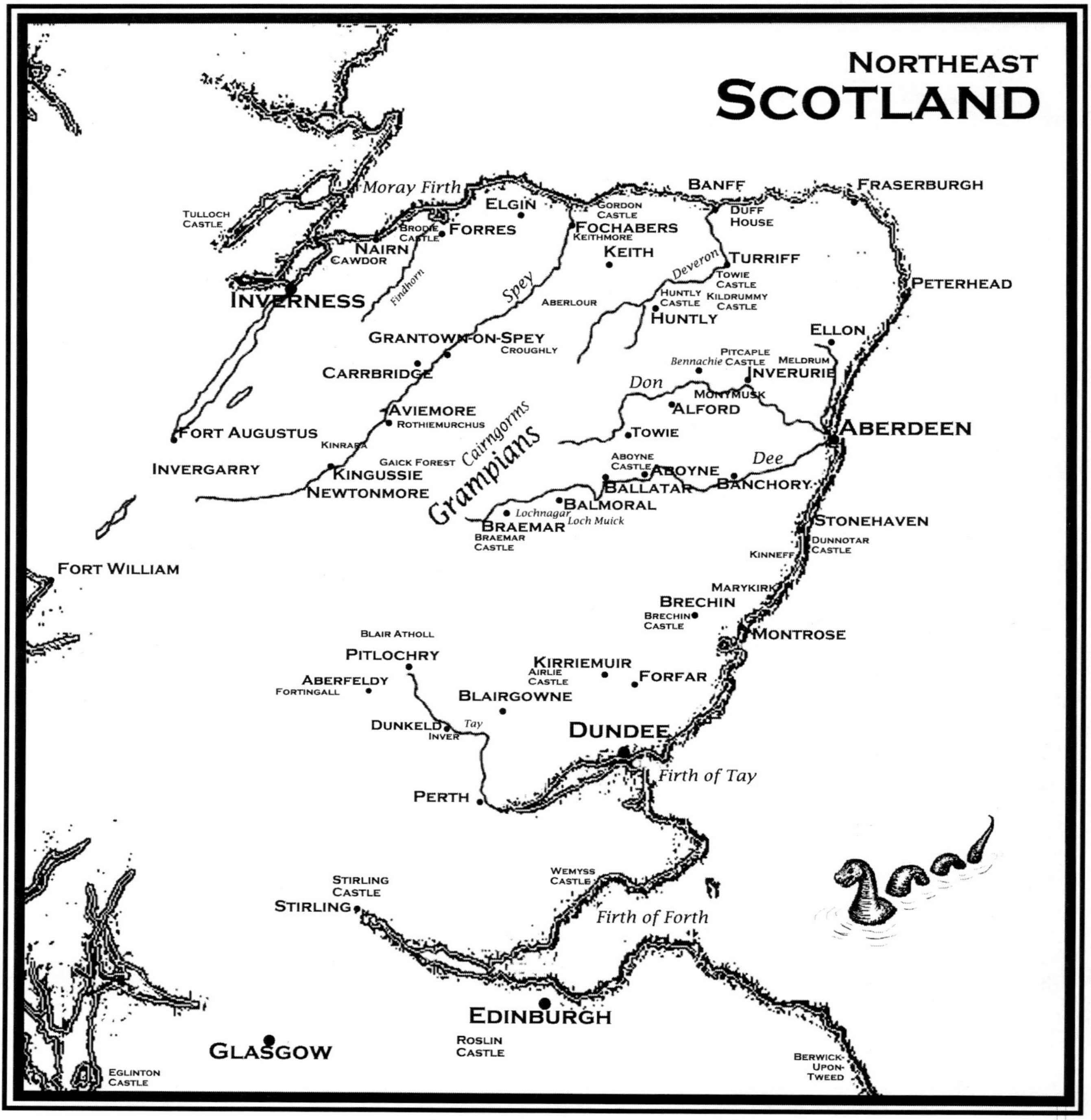

NORTHEAST
SCOTLAND
Moray Firth
Tulloch Castle
Elgin
Banff
Fraserburgh
Gordon Castle
Duff House
Brodie Castle
Forres
Fochabers
Keithmore
Nairn
Cawdor
Keith
Turriff
Deveron
Findhorn
Spey
Towie Castle
Huntly Castle
Kildrummy Castle
Peterhead
Inverness
Aberlour
Huntly
Ellon
Grantown-on-Spey
Croughly
Pitcaple
Bennachie Castle
Meldrum
Carrbridge
Inverurie
Don
Monymusk
Alford
Aviemore
Rothiemurchus
Cairngorms
Fort Augustus
Towie
Aberdeen
Kinrara
Grampians
Aboyne Castle
Aboyne
Dee
Invergarry
Gaick Forest
Kingussie
Ballatar
Banchory
Newtonmore
Balmoral
Lochnagar
Stonehaven
Braemar
Loch Muick
Braemar Castle
Dunnotar Castle
Kinneff
Fort William
Marykirk
Brechin
Brechin Castle
Montrose
Blair Atholl
Pitlochry
Kirriemuir
Airlie Castle
Aberfeldy
Forfar
Fortingall
Blairgowne
Dunkeld
Tay
Inver
Dundee
Firth of Tay
Perth
Wemyss Castle
Stirling Castle
Stirling
Firth of Forth
Edinburgh
Roslin Castle
Glasgow
Eglinton Castle
Berwick-Upon-Tweed

The Music of Spey

Strathspey. For many, the word is a mystifying mouthful of sounds. For Scottish dancers and musicians, it means a unique and beautiful kind of dance, and the type of tune that accompanies it. For people living in Scotland, it's the region near the River Spey, full of woodlands, mountains, craggy hills, farms, wild streams, castles and ruins. Like the region of Strathspey, the tunes called strathspeys have multiple personalities: rugged and gritty; lyrical and emotional; calm and pastoral; spiky and fierce.

This collection of strathspeys started life as a tunebook for some of my fiddle students. It kept growing as I found tunes I liked to play for concerts, or for dances, or just for fun. Having an inquiring mind, I wanted to know the stories behind some of the titles, so several years ago I started making notes about the more interesting ones I found.

And then I had a wild thought, "Why not make a collection of these tunes (as dozens of Scottish fiddlers and editors have done for a couple of hundred years now), and see if other people would be interested in this, too?" It seems timely. Websites about Scottish and Celtic music abound (with both good and erroneous information); people are interested in this kind of music and want to find out more about it.

So, this book is a labor of love. I love playing strathspeys, love hearing them played well, love watching dancers move to them. And I love sharing tunes with other people who would like them, too. If you are reading this, you are probably one of them.

You might be a violinist or fiddler; you might play the harp, or a wind instrument, or a piano or accordion, or you might simply be interested in listening to the music and reading about the tunes. If you are a violinist, don't be alarmed about my use of "fiddle" almost interchangeably with "violin"; in my thinking, they are exactly the same instrument. It's the style of playing that differs.

I need to say, first, that this is **not** intended to be a scholarly book. There are many good scholarly books, and you can find them listed in my "Sources" at the back of this collection. I have a lot of them on my desk. Many of the old, public domain ones are e-books on my computer. This book is not meant to be anything but my own notebook of tunes that I think are interesting, with some stories and history about them, following in the steps of many compilers who have done the same thing. There are thousands of strathspeys out there, old and new; as I was putting this book together, I kept thinking, "Oh, wait, what about that one—that's such a great tune!" That way lies madness, and a *really* long book. So I have tried to stay with tunes in the public domain that may be fun to play—some quirky, some straightforward, some difficult, some well known, some not —and have resisted the urge to put in every tune I know or meet. They are arranged (roughly) in chronological order, with early and traditional tunes first.

You can listen to all of the tunes in this collection at the following website: **www.melbay.com/22123EB**. It helps to learn a tune at a slower tempo at first. There are many good software programs that allow you to slow the speed of a recording so you can practice along with the music.

Playing Strathspeys

I'm a fiddle player. I learned to play strathspeys by playing them for Scottish country dances, and with a lot of help from some excellent musicians who have been playing for a lot longer than I. It's not easy to find someone who can show you how to play tunes well for dancers, and I really value the help from my mentors. That's part of the reason I wanted to record each of these strathspeys, so others could listen to the tunes and get a feel for them. Having said that, there are many excellent musicians out there who can play these tunes well, and they might have a little different interpretation of them than I have. That's the fun of traditional music—it's shared by a community of players, and each one brings something different to the tune; each one teaches you something you might not have thought of before.

There have been books and essays written about playing strathspeys in the past 150 years or so that have good information and advice for players. In 1922, William C. Honeyman, a fiddler, teacher, and competition judge, published an enjoyable piece called "Strathspey Players Past and Present," offering historical background as well as some strong opinions. Earlier, in 1898, he wrote *The Strathspey, Reel, and Hornpipe Tutor*, with some straightforward dance sets, and detailed bowings. He was writing after the strathspey had been popular for nearly 200 years, and was something of an expert in the field himself. In his book, he gives copious and careful instructions to players; at the end of it all, however, he admits that "no two strathspey players play the same tune exactly alike."

He does, though, point out cardinal qualities that make a good strathspey player: "1st, freedom of bowing; 2nd, intonation; and 3rd, spirit and expression." These take work and much listening to achieve, but it's a reachable goal, even if you haven't had the music in your ears since childhood.

Bowing

The strathspey evolved from the 4/4 meter reel, played slower than a reel, with dotted rhythms (*looong-short, looong-short*) rather than a steady stream of equal eighth notes. In fact, early strathspeys were called "strathspey reels" in many collections, and in some cases were not notated any differently from reels. The editor might sometimes put something like, "in accented strathspey style" at the beginning of the tune, or sometimes merely "Strathspey." People often ask how strathspeys are different from hornpipes, also a 4/4 type of tune, somewhat slower than a reel. Hornpipes also can have a dotted rhythm, but it is always the *long-short* pattern. Strathspeys, though, use a pair of dotted figures—long-short, short-long—to make the characteristic "Scots snap" that gives the tune energy and pulse:

For fiddle players, the bowing for Scots snaps is what gives it the kick, the air beneath the wings. Here's another variation of the snap:

For this type of snap, the "up-driven" bow style made famous by Niel Gow in the early 18th century makes the snap light, crisp, and powerful. The first sixteenth note is on a down-bow, near the tip; the next three notes are all on the same up-bow, and it is this kind of "driven" up-bow stroke that lifts dancers' feet off the floor and gives strathspeys their characteristic edginess and drive.

For more about bowing, James Hunter's *The Fiddle Music of Scotland,* edited by Alastair Hardie and William Hardie, has an excellent introductory section that discusses bowing techniques at some length.

Ornamentation

The melody as written on these pages is the skeleton of the tune, without much additional information like bowings, dynamics, and articulations. What good Scottish fiddlers do to add the Scottish idiom to the music is often not written down, and in fact, is often not ever done the same way twice. Many collections will attempt to show grace notes, triplets and birls, double-stops and chords, unison notes, and other kinds of ornaments, which may be helpful, but in truth, it's often the editor's addition to the original tune, and it is sometimes better just to listen to someone who knows the idiom, playing the tune well. Rarely does a tune appear precisely the same way in more than one collection; each editor or compiler adds his or her own touch to it by notating what they think is appropriate ornamentation, articulation, and phrasing. To really learn the music, play good, traditional recordings over and over again; sing the tunes out loud; get the feel of the phrasing and ornaments in your ears and fingers. It's a lot like a language—listen, imitate, listen some more, play...it will come to you.

You may notice when you listen to recordings that not only is it true that "no two strathspey players play the same tune exactly alike," as Honeyman said, but that no one player plays the tune the same way twice! What is on the page of music is a guideline; the player often uses creative judgment to vary the tune's melody a bit. You may notice that snaps are sometimes omitted, and often replaced by a triplet (also called a "doodle," or birl). ***Note:*** *the "triplet" as Scottish fiddlers know it is actually more like two sixteenth notes and an eighth note, not three even notes.* Part of the trouble with reading ornaments on a page of Scottish music is that it's not a science. A good reader and trained musician not familiar with the Scottish idiom, playing from a printed page of strathspeys, will read it exactly "right," but it may not sound exactly Scottish. Folk musicians often take some liberties with what is written on the page. A fiddler might change octaves, or play an adjacent open string with the bow and "drone" on that string for a bit, or use double-stops (more than one note played at one time). What is possible to play, of course, depends on the instrument—for example, a flute would not be able to play more than one note at a time, or play below middle C. Improvisation is sometimes needed!

Traditional Scottish Fiddling, A Player's Guide, compiled by Christine Martin, has an in-depth section on both ornamentation and bowing.

Types of Strathspeys

There is a lot of discussion about this topic, with people often dividing up strathspeys into as many as seven categories. In general, you will find strathspeys falling into these groups:

Song, or pastoral strathspeys: Smoother than strathspeys falling into the "strong" or "lyrical" category; not so much emphasis on snaps, although there are often a few, and you may want to add a few here and there as you think tasteful. They often sound like they might have lyrics, and many of them do, particularly the Robert Burns songs that are very popular. Some examples might be "Mary Morrison," "O Were I On Parnassus Hill," and "The Music of Spey."

Strong and lyrical strathspeys: These are tunes with much forward momentum, with a powerful surge on the first beat of each measure. Strong strathspeys typically have a lot of snaps, perhaps runs of triplets and sixteenth notes, and feel angular and edgy, to be played "with fire and force," as James Scott Skinner said. One of my teachers commented to me, "Put some dirt in it! These kinds of strathspeys aren't pretty!" They're full of life and gritty reality. Examples of strong strathspeys might be "Aboyne Castle," by Peter Milne, "Lady Burnside's Birthday," by Charles Duff, or "The North Side of Spey," by Charles Grant. Lyrical strathspeys, too, can be strong, but they can be played poignantly and emotionally, and they usually don't seem as edgy. Some examples of lyrical strathspeys might be "Banks of Spey," "Invercauld's," "Mr. A. G. Wilkins," and "Keithmore."

Schottische-like strathspeys: These are bouncy tunes with a lot of vertical motion, not so much forward drive as a strong strathspey. Examples might be "Braes o' Tullymet," "Haughs of Cromdale," and "Brechin Castle."

You may also hear people talking about ***"bagpipe strathspeys,"*** like "Devil in the Kitchen," and "John McNiell's Highland Fling." These are often written in a modal scale used by bagpipes (A mixolydian, without the G sharp normally found in A major), and they have much vertical, bouncy motion.

Strathspey Tempo

In many early tune collections, the composers or editors marked tunes as "slow," "accented strathspey style," "dance tempo," and other vaguely descriptive phrases. For dancing, strathspeys are probably best played between 104 and 112 beats per minute, which allows the dancers to move well and gracefully without either falling over or scurrying around to get where they need to be. The best rule of thumb is to watch the dancers and adjust accordingly. For concerts and performances, the "slow" tempo marking is subjective, but important—the strathspey becomes more a slow air, and the musician can play it with feeling and tenderness.

Examples of slow, or performance strathspeys might be "Roslin Castle," "Grieg's Strathspey," "The Marchioness of Cornwallis," by William Marshall, and "The Marchioness of Huntly," in Bb major, also by Marshall. Some tunes are designated by early composers as "slow when not danced," and Marshall very clearly noted that his Bb version of "The Marchioness of Huntly" was for performance, presumably slower; for dancing, it should be played in A major (and the fermata in measure 5 of the B part would be omitted).

It is fairly intimidating to imagine publishing a collection of tunes simply because one likes them. There are so many collections out in the world, and there are so many people who know far about Scottish music and its history than I. Yet I keep thinking there is a need for this kind of collection, one that presents only one type of tune, and that tries to present the tunes in some kind of historical and cultural context. I hope that you enjoy trying the tunes, reading about them, and listening to the recordings.

If I had to list all the people to whom I am deeply indebted for information, help, and support, I doubt the publisher could grant me enough pages to do so. At the very least, I need to acknowledge the people I have studied and played music with and learned much from—Bobby Brown, Alasdair Fraser, Patsy Reid, Dave Wiesler, Elke Baker, Liz Donaldson, Laura Risk, Nicholas Williams, Pete Campbell, Ted Ehrhard, Dean Herington, Muriel Johnstone, Earl Gaddis, Brian Reagin, David DiGiuseppe, Roger Gold, Celia Wright, Julie Gorka, Laura Lengnick, Anne Taylor. Friends made along the way are too numerous to mention individually, but all have had important roles in this effort, and I could not have done anything on this scale without them. Special thanks to John, my dear friend and husband, who has put up with hearing hundreds of strathspeys played for the past year or two, and still doesn't seem to mind.

Julie Gorka was kind enough to play all of these tunes (and many more that didn't make it into this book), and provide chords that would be accessible to most players and instruments. They are, of course, only one way to hear the melody, and you may want to interpret the harmonies differently. The chords are straightforward; however, note that chords with a slash (for example, A/E) specify a bass note (in that example, an A major chord with an E in the bass). Accompanists may choose to ignore the slash chords, or come up with an entirely different arrangement; these chords are just to help get you started. In some cases, I have added a comment at the end of a tune, to "resolve to a D chord" (or E chord, or whatever) indicating that the tune ends rather up in the air; for these kinds of tunes you may want to add on a final measure to come back to the tonic, or home chord.

Lisa McDonald created the illustrations and the map of Scotland, always enthusiastic and cheerful (even excited!) about coming up with more ideas and concepts, and she has now started playing strathspeys on her fiddle...

A New Strathspey Reel

G major / E minor

James Oswald, 1710–1769

Written by James Oswald, this may be the earliest printed strathspey. It appeared in Volume III of Oswald's multi-volume collection, *The Caledonian Pocket Companion*, in about 1745.

James Oswald lived in Edinburgh for several years, and advertised himself as a "violinist, organist, composer, and teacher of dancing." He belonged to a society of musicians called The Temple of Apollo, and may have published many of his compositions either anonymously, or under the pseudonym David Rizzio. In 1741, he moved to London, and in 1743, began compiling *The Caledonian Pocket Companion*, a project that spanned over 15 years and included more than 500 tunes.

Benjamin Franklin toured Scotland in 1759, and stayed with Lord Kames at Blair Drummond in Stirling. He later wrote to Lord Kames that old Scottish airs, especially as played by James Oswald on his violincello, needed no harmony or ornamentation—the tunes brought "tears of pleasure in the eyes of his auditors."

Part of the appeal of this tune is its "dark side"—how it easily slips from G major to E minor, like the underside of a leaf blowing in the wind.

Ruffian's Rant

D major

Possibly composed by Niel Gow, 1727–1807

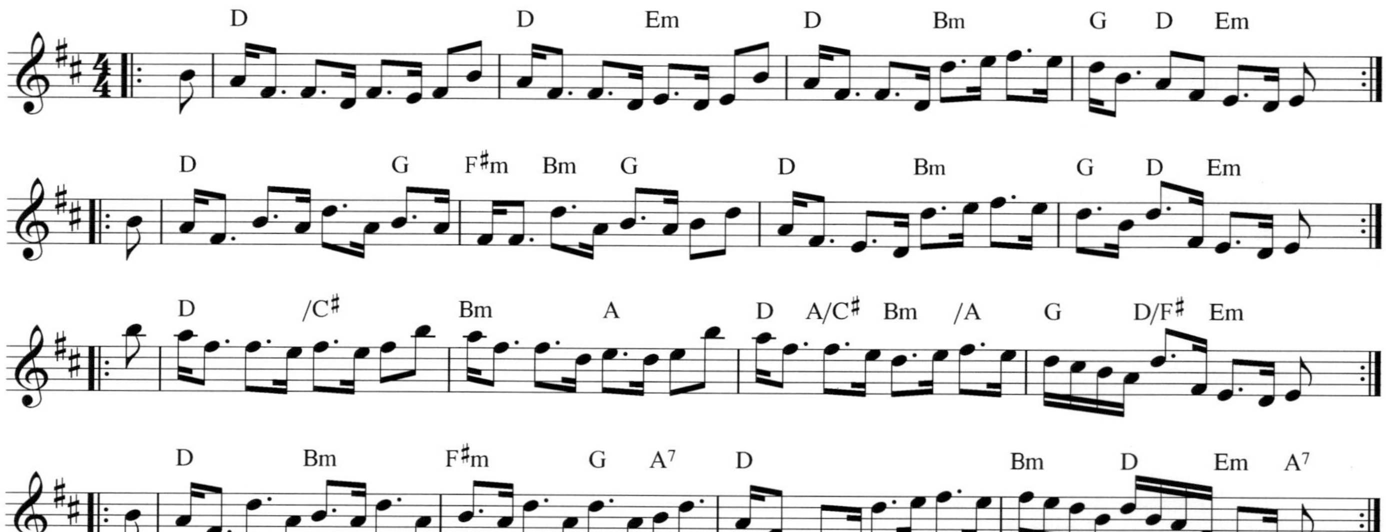

Last time: resolve to D
on a final bow chord

The tune "Ruffian's Rant" was published by Robert Bremner in one of the early collections of Scottish dance music, in 1765, and also in the *Scots Musical Museum* (1787–1803), a collection with which Robert Burns was much involved. The tune was probably written around 1742, and is often attributed to Niel Gow (1727–1807)—but no one knows for certain.

The melody is used for a traditional Scots song with words by Elizabeth Grant (1745–1814), "Roy's Wife of Aldivalloch."

"Ruffian's Rant" in Bremner's collection

Roslin Castle

C minor

Traditional; printed as "House of Glamis" in Wm. McGibbon's 2nd Collection, 1746. Possibly composed by James Oswald, 1710–1769.

Roslin Castle
walls and gates

This tune is hauntingly beautiful when played slowly, not for dancing. It is sometimes played for Scottish country dances, but it seems more suitable as a listening piece. It was also well known as a march during the American Revolutionary War period, played by British troops (many of whom were Scots from the Highlands) as they left the town now called Roslyn, Long Island, in New York. The original Roslin Castle (and nearby Rosslyn Chapel, with its magnificent carvings) still stands just south of Edinburgh, famous as a much-haunted 14th-century ruin with a long history of ghost stories. It is the setting for Sir Walter Scott's poem, "Rosabelle":

—O'er Roslin all that dreary night
A wondrous blaze was seen to gleam;
'Twas broader than the watch-fire's light,
And redder than the bright moonbeam…

The Earl and Countess of Rosslyn still own the property, and live in a house built at the heart of the ancient castle.

One of the musical angels
in Rosslyn Chapel

The Ewie wi' the Crooked Horn

G minor

Attributed by Simon Fraser to Mr. Rose of Kilravock, Mr. Campbell of Budyet, and Mr. Sutherland of Kinsteary, early 1700s

Many versions of this tune appear in collections from the past couple of centuries. This is the version from Fraser's 1816 collection—a little quirky, a little odd, but interesting. You might think this old traditional strathspey is about a mere sheep, but it's not. In his collection, *The Airs and Melodies Peculiar to the Highlands of Scotland and The Isles*, Captain Simon Fraser notes that this is part of a set of tunes put together by three gentlemen from Nairnshire, "eminent performers," in about 1715. He goes on to say, "The ewe thus celebrated is no other than the whisky still, with its crooked horn, which gave more milk than all the sheep in the country."

Still life with ewe

However it came to be, it is an old favorite, to be played with spirit.

Laird of Brodie

D major

Attributed by Simon Fraser to Mr. Rose of Kilravock, Mr. Campbell of Budyet, and Mr. Sutherland of Kinsteary, early 1700s

This is a slow strathspey, to be played expressively. Simon Fraser printed it in his *Airs and Melodies Peculiar to the Highlands of Scotland and the Isles* (1816), with a syntactically puzzling note that had appeared originally with the tune:

> This tune supposed to be composed by the roving King James would spread among all his subjects as his production, but I find the best sett of it preserved in the Highlands and sung to Gaelic words.

Fraser goes on to say that although the general assumption is that the "roving King James" was the composer, it is more likely that the tune was set by the same three Nairnshire gentlemen who are responsible for the setting of the "Ewie with the Crooked Horn." They would have written it in honor of their neighbor, the Laird of Brodie, perhaps Alexander Brodie (1698–1754), Member of Parliament. The Laird's family tried to stay neutral during the Jacobite - Stuart conflicts; Brodie later spoke out in Parliament against the ban on wearing kilts.

Brodie Castle is between the towns of Nairn and Forres, not far from Inverness, and was the home of the Brodie family until the 1980s. It is now open to the public and maintained by the National Trust for Scotland.

Panmure House / Miss Lyall

A minor

Traditional

Many traditional tunes ("traditional" meaning no one is sure who wrote it) have multiple names, depending on what an editor might have decided to call a tune in an early printed collection. This strong strathspey has appeared in many collections, under both titles. "Panmure House" was a magnificent and ancient estate and manor house that was demolished in the 1950s. "Miss Lyall" was very likely Mrs. Anne Grant of Laggan (1755–1838), a novelist and poet who lived in the Strathspey region most of her life.

Old picture of Panmure House, from a postcard

Grieg's Strathspey

G minor

Traditional

This haunting tune appears in the keys of G minor or A minor, depending on what collection of tunes you find it in. It is a slow strathspey; J. Scott Skinner calls it a "Pastoral," and "an Ancient Melody," and notes it as Nathaniel Gow's favorite strathspey. Skinner's version is in G minor. In *The Skye Collection*, it is in A minor, to be played "slow," and is noted as "very old."

One reason that Skinner, an excellent violinist, might have played "Grieg's" in G minor is that, for fiddle players, it lends itself very well to using harmonics on the final Gs of each strain.

Beauty of the North

Eb major

Traditional

This beautiful tune is from Captain Simon Fraser's collection, The *Airs and Melodies Peculiar to the Highlands of Scotland and the Isles,* published in 1816. Captain Fraser was a talented fiddler, and he wrote many excellent tunes. His father and grandfather were both highly musical, both of them being singers and collectors of Gaelic songs. Fraser learned many of the tunes in the *Airs and Melodies* from them, as he frequently notes in the collection's Appendix. It is quite possible that he composed "The Beauty of the North"; however, as he was often vague about the source of many of the tunes in the collection, that mystery will likely remain unsolved.

Birks of Invermay
(Scotland's First James)

G major

Traditional

This lyrical, singing melody was published in William Thomson's *Orpheus Caledonius*, an early collection from 1733. It was also known as "Scotland's First James," and appears under that title in the *Gesto Collection of Highland Music* (1895). In some collections it is not in G, but in Bb major.

King James I, "Scotland's first James," was considered a master musician, as Keith Norman MacDonald, the editor of the *Gesto Collection*, says in a footnote to the tune. He may have composed some ancient tunes that have come down to us as "traditional."

Invermay (or Endermay, as it sometimes appears) is a lovely wooded glen not far from the River Earn, outside of Perth, and the "birks" are birch trees.

Braes o' Tullymet

G minor

Traditional

The "braes of Tullymet" (or Tulliemet, as it sometimes appears on modern signposts) is a hilly, upland area between Dunkeld and Inver, Aberfeldy, and Pitlochry, about 30 miles northwest of Dundee. It was the birthplace of Robert Mackintosh, the fiddler and composer nicknamed "Red Rob" because he had brilliantly red hair. The Mackintoshes were a musical family—Robert's brother, a blacksmith in a small village nearby, had several children and grandchildren who were all fiddlers. One of the grandsons, James Mackintosh (1801–1873), became a violin-maker, and was a pupil of Peter Hardie ("Highland Hardie"), also a good violin-maker and fiddler living in the Tullymet area. Peter Hardie was a pupil of Niel Gow, who was from nearby Dunkeld, and often played music with him; Hardie is buried in a graveyard in Dowally, one of the many villages in the braes of Tullymet.

Red Rob Mackintosh was born in Tullymet in 1745; he left there in 1773 for Edinburgh, where he taught violin. One of his pupils there was Niel Gow's son, Nathaniel. He later moved to Aberdeen, and then to London, where he died in 1807.

Ferintosh

D major

Traditional

Capt. Simon Fraser's 1816 collection, *The Airs and Melodies Peculiar to the Highlands of Scotland and the Isles,* includes this strathspey. Fraser noted that the tune celebrates the district of Ferintosh, "so famous for the production of the genuine Highland beverage, called whisky." Ferintosh is in the Highland region of Ross and Cromartie.

Fraser does not take credit for composing this somewhat quirky, unusual tune; some accounts, however, suggest that he might have written it.

The Fir Tree

D major

Traditional

Many strathspeys were written to honor people or places, often for wealthy patrons who appreciated having their names or houses immortalized in a piece of music. Not so common are titles that capture a bit of nature. This slightly odd, quirky tune was an early printed strathspey; it appeared in Robert Bremner's *Collection of Scots Reels or Country Dances* (1765).

Tunes printed in early collections were sometimes not clearly marked as to whether they should be played fast or slow, or even if they were meant to be reels or strathspeys. In Bremner's collection, he labeled each tune as "Strathspey" to make it clear that it is to have the dotted rhythm and the snaps associated with that type of tune. For "The Fir Tree," Bremner also added a note: "N.B. The Strathspey Reels are play'd much slower than the others."

The Strathspey region was known for large forests of fir; the logs were harvested and were floated down the River Spey to the sawmills at Garmouth.

Haughs of Cromdale

A minor

Traditional

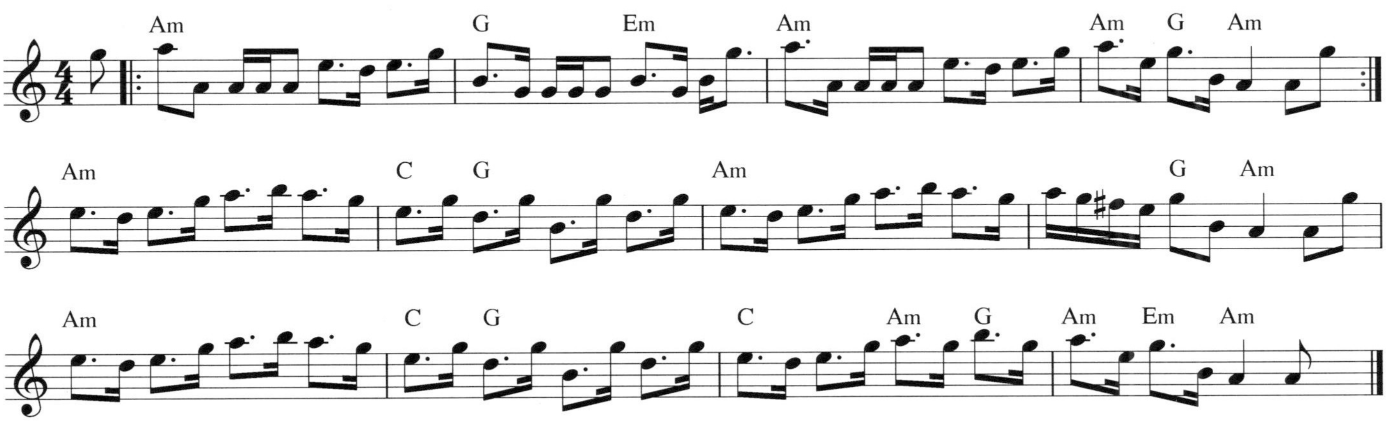

This is another old Highland tune with a story. Donald Grant (1760–1839) noted it as "old" in his collection, where it was first printed. There is a ballad that goes with it, describing the resounding defeat of the Highlanders on the 1st of May, 1690, in a battle fought on the haughs—areas of flat ground, near a river. The song appears in James Hogg's *Jacobite Relics* (1819). Interestingly, over the intervening years, the lyrics seemed to blend in one story people who were 40 years apart in history, making the ballad wildly inaccurate. Nonetheless, the tune that accompanied the lyrics was spirited and gutsy, and has served to inspire people to acts of courage ever since.

The site of the battle at the Haughs of Cromdale is on the banks of the River Spey, near Grantown-on-Spey.

The tune appears in A minor or E minor in different collections. This version is from Donald Grant's *Collection of Strathspeys, Reels, Jigs, &c* (c. 1790).

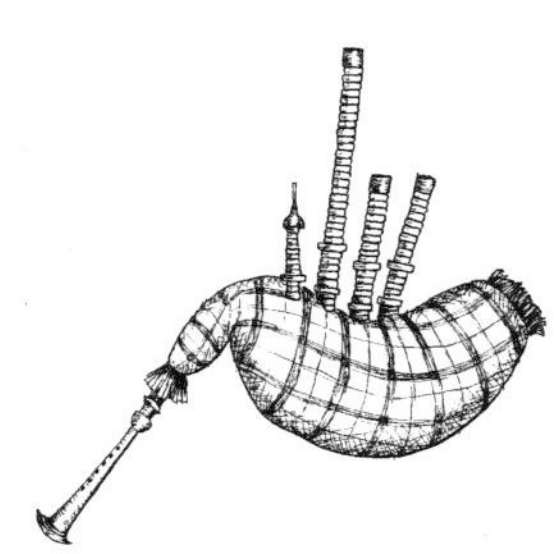

Hawthorn Tree of Cawdor

A minor

Traditional

Simon Fraser surmises that this tune was written by a Mr. Campbell of Budyet, and mentions that the tune was considered "old" by Mr. Gow.

A wonderful legend is at the heart of late 14th-century Cawdor Castle, also associated (erroneously) with the historical Macbeth. The tale of how it came to be built centers around a donkey and a tree: the Thane of Cawdor, who had a small castle nearby, decided he would build a larger, stronger tower. He had a dream that told him how to find a good site for the tower, and he followed the instructions in that dream to the letter. He loaded a chest of gold on the back of a donkey and let it roam around the area for a day. Where the donkey lay down to rest in the evening, wherever it might be, would be the site for the new castle. At the end of the day, the donkey lay down under a hawthorn tree.

And around that tree was built Cawdor Castle. Today, you can visit the castle, walk into the ground floor guardroom, which protected the approach to the castle drawbridge, and see what is left of the ancient hawthorn, standing in the center of the room. Actually, recent analysis of the wood identifies the tree as a holly (but still a "thorn" tree). Nonetheless, radiocarbon dating of the tree gives the date of about AD 1372, the approximate time the castle was built. Both hollies and hawthorns were considered magical—both were sacred trees in Celtic groves. "Freshness to the hawthorn tree of Cawdor!" is still used to wish prosperity to the house of Cawdor.

Highlands of Banffshire

F major

Traditional

The Highlands of Banffshire have been famous for centuries for their wild beauty and amazing scenery, some of it bleak and wildly desolate, some thickly forested, with untamed rivers. They are known as excellent hunting grounds and deer forests. The area south of the River Spey—the Gordon estates and holdings—was especially prized for the richness of its wildlife and forest lands.

Simon Fraser included this dramatic-sounding tune in his *Airs and Melodies Peculiar to the Highlands of Scotland and the Isles* (1816), and writes:

> The Highlands of Banffshire, extending south of the Spey, have been long famous for the best dancers of the strathspeys, which must have been well performed to inspire them sufficiently. In this district also lie the most picturesque scenery, the finest sporting grounds and deer forests, perhaps in Great Britain, belonging to the Duke of Gordon, Earl of Fife, &c., long inaccessible to strangers, from the badness of the roads, and want of bridges.

Cutting Ferns (Pulling Bracken)

A minor

Traditional

This is an old strathspey, originating from the "mouth music," or *puirt a beul* tradition of the Highlands and Hebrides. (Pronounce "puirt a beul" roughly as "poorsht-a-beel.") Tunes like these were work songs, sung to accompany tasks like weaving or fulling cloth. The work was rhythmic, as are the tunes that gave momentum to the workers.

This beautiful tune has appeared in many guises—as a jig, a reel, a polka, an air—but it is a lovely strathspey that works for dancing as well as listening. It has several titles: "Pulling Bracken," "Cutting Ferns," and its Gaelic title, "Tha mi sgìth," meaning "I am tired," from the first line of the lyrics to the traditional Gaelic song:

> I am tired, on my own,
> pulling bracken, pulling bracken,
> I am tired, and on my own,
> pulling bracken, always.

Why pull bracken? Bracken is a type of large fern that has spread widely over the pasturelands and hillsides of Scotland; it is poisonous to livestock like cattle, sheep, pigs and horses. Unfortunately, the only good way to get rid of it is to cut it down, or pull it out. But it's a tough plant, and very hard on the hands.

This version of the tune is from the *Athole Collection* (1884).

Strath-Spè

E minor

Traditional

Haunting, melancholy, perhaps a little wintry-sounding—this strathspey carries simply the title of the region, "Strath-spè" (with the emphasis on the second syllable). The subtitle added by Captain Simon Fraser is "The Native Country of the Sprightly Dance." He printed it in his *Airs and Melodies Peculiar to the Highlands of Scotland and the Isles* in 1816, and he comments:

> In passing through the district of Strathspey, the traveller may be apt to forget, that among the long ranges of firwood and heath on each side, originated that sprightly style of performing and dancing the music which bears its name, now in universal request from the Spey to the Ganges.

The tune is marked to be played, "slow strathspey style," probably indicating it pulls on the heartstrings more as an air than as a dance tune. For all of the tunes in his collection, Fraser adds dynamic markings, slurs, and articulations (which are omitted in this more-or-less "plain" representation of the tune), as some compilers and editors did. In this tune he also added double-stops (two notes to be played simultaneously), which could be played or left out at the discretion of the performer. The tune also requires a fiddler to leave first position and play in third position, which was somewhat unusual for most strathspeys.

Clach na Cudain

D major

Traditional

This is as strong and solid a tune as its name. "Clach na Cudain" can be translated as the "Key Stone of Inverness," one of the foundation stones of the city of Inverness, near the Market Cross where all business was transacted, and where people gathered to hear news and gossip. It was also known as the "stone of tubs." Captain Simon Fraser, in his explanatory notes to the tune, wrote that "it was formerly the resting place of the servant girls, in bringing their water-pails from the river…a celebrated rendezvous for obtaining all the news and scandal imaginable."

Legend has it that Inverness will survive as long as the key stone remains intact.

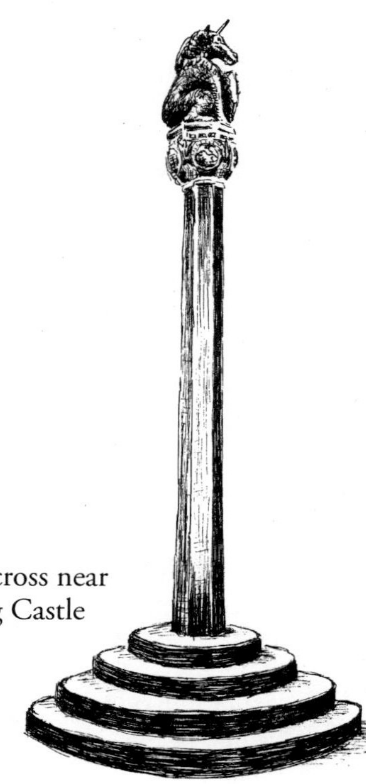

Market cross near Stirling Castle

Let's to the Ard

F major

Traditional

Loch Ard is a small, beautiful lake, lying between Loch Lomond and Loch Katrine, about 25 miles north of Glasgow. Its sheltered location, high up in the hills near Ben Lomond, have for centuries made it a lovely spot for hiking, fishing, quiet boating, and wildlife observation. It is also the source for the River Forth.

"Let's to the Ard" was printed in Robert Bremner's *Collection of Scots Reels or Country Dances* (1765).

The feisty capercaillie, now a threatened species in Scotland, can occasionally be seen in the forests around Loch Ard.

Rothemurches Rant

C major

Traditional

Robert Bremner printed this tune in his 1765 collection. Robert Burns liked this tune very much, and set his song, "Lassie wi' the lint-white locks" to it. He wrote, "I am just now making verses for Rothemurche's Rant, an air which puts me in raptures…[it] is an air both original and beautiful." It appears in many collections in slightly different forms, sometimes in the key of C, sometimes in D.

Robert Mackintosh's version is more ornate than the one in Bremner's, and he includes many more variations. J. Scott Skinner puts it in D, as "the key that seems best to suit the character of the tune," and "as played by Peter Milne." It's a lovely tune, whatever key you choose.

Athol Cummers

E minor

Traditional

A very early printed strathspey, this tune was printed in Robert Bremner's *Collection of Scots Reels and Country Dances* (1765). The structure of the tune has varied with different collections. In Bremner's edition, it's a four-part tune, but doesn't have the usual 16- or 32-bar structure that many strathspeys have. The first two strains (the A and B parts) are 4 bars each, which is expected; the last two strains (the C and D parts) are 6 bars each, making this a rather quirky, interesting, and crooked tune!

James Hogg, a poet and fiddler who lived in the late 18th and early 19th century, published a book of songs called *The Forest Minstrel, a selection of songs, adapted to the most favourite Scottish airs*. He tells of one evening when he was "sawing away on the fiddle with great energy and elevation" and playing "the strathspey called 'Athol Cummers'." His mother called out to him, "Dear Jimmie, are there ony words to that tune?" He replied, "No that ever I heard, mother." She said, "O man, it's a shame to hear sic a good tune an' nae words till't. Gae away ben the house, like a good lad, and mak' me a verse till't." He did so, and wrote verses about the "Athol cummers"—the lovely girls from Athol.

When the fickle lasses vex me,
When the cares o' life perplex me,
When I'm fley'd wi' frightfu' rumours,
Then I lilt o' Athol cummers.
Tis my cure for a' disasters,
Kebbit ewes an/ crabbit masters,
Drifty nights an' dripping summers—
A' my joy is Athol cummers!

Don Side

G major

Traditional

This is an early four-part printed strathspey. It appeared in Robert Bremner's 1765 *Collection of Scots Reels or Country Dances* (this version is from his collection), and also in Angus Cumming's *Collection of Strathspeys or Old Highland Reels* (about 1780).

The River Don rises from the Cairngorms, not far from Lochnagar, and meanders eastward to Aberdeen, passing Towie Castle, Alford, Monymusk, and Inverurie.

Invercauld's

A minor

Traditional

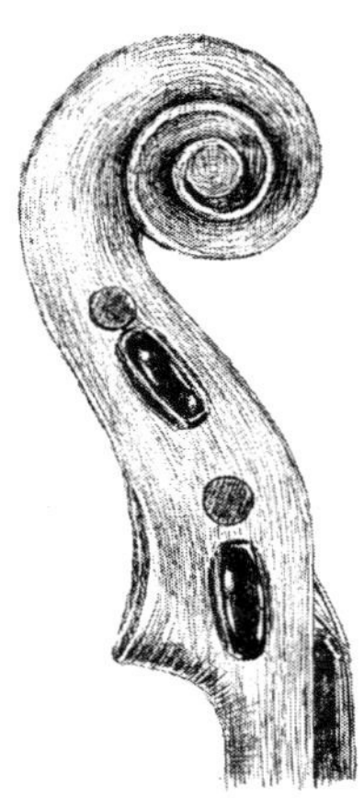

This tune appears in several collections, perhaps the earliest one being as "Invercald's Reell," in Angus Cumming's *Collection of Strathspey or Old Highland Reels by Angus Cumming at Grantown in Strathspey, 1780.* Robert Petrie, in his *Second Collection of Strathspey Reels and Country Dances* (1795–96), also publishes the tune. In that collection, it appears as "Invercauld's Reel," and shows no sign of any dotted eighth and sixteenth notes, very often the most obvious evidence that a tune is meant to be a strathspey. Many composers and publishers of the 18th century, however, still used the term "strathspey reel," and did not always set the tune with dotted rhythms. By the time it appeared in *The Athole Collection*, however, in 1884, it was typeset as a strathspey, with a full complement of snaps and ornaments.

"Invercauld's" is another one of those strathspeys with momentum and grace, to be played with strength, but it leaves room for quieter, tender phrasing, too.

They Stole My Wife from Me Last Night
(Ghoid iad mo bhean uam reir)

A minor

Traditional

This very rich, old tune can be plaintive, when played slowly as an air, and it can be a wonderful Scottish country dance tune that goes well with a song strathspey set. It is introspective, but it has strength and some bite to it, too. It was published in Patrick McDonald's *Collection of Highland Vocal Airs never hitherto published, to which are added a few of the most lively Country Dances or Reels of the North Highlands and Western Isles* (1781); he notes that it is "an ancient air."

Waulking of the Fauld

A minor

Traditional

This lovely, somewhat melancholy strathspey is an old tune, perhaps a Highland song. The melody was around before the poet Allan Ramsay (1686–1758) wrote lyrics for it that appeared in his play, *The Gentle Shepherd*, in the 1720s. The title appears as "The Wauking of the Fauld" or "The Wawking of the Faulds" (meaning keeping watch over a sheep fold). The words for it in *The Gentle Shepherd* provide the alternate title for it, "My Peggy is a young thing":

> My Peggy is a young thing,
> And I'm not very auld,
> Yet well I like to meet her at
> The wawking of the fauld.

The strathspey also appears in James Oswald's *Caledonian Pocket Companion, Book 3* (c. 1745), and in *The Athole Collection of the Dance Music of Scotland* (1884).

The Mill Mill O

D major

Traditional

Both this tune and "O Were I On Parnassus Hill" are song strathspeys, being melodies that Robert Burns used as an accompaniment to his poems. Song strathspeys often do not have as many "Scots snaps" as other kinds of strathspeys; they tend to be smoother (although it doesn't hurt to add a few snaps now and then, as appropriate, to keep things from getting too smooth).

O Were I On Parnassus Hill

E minor

Traditional

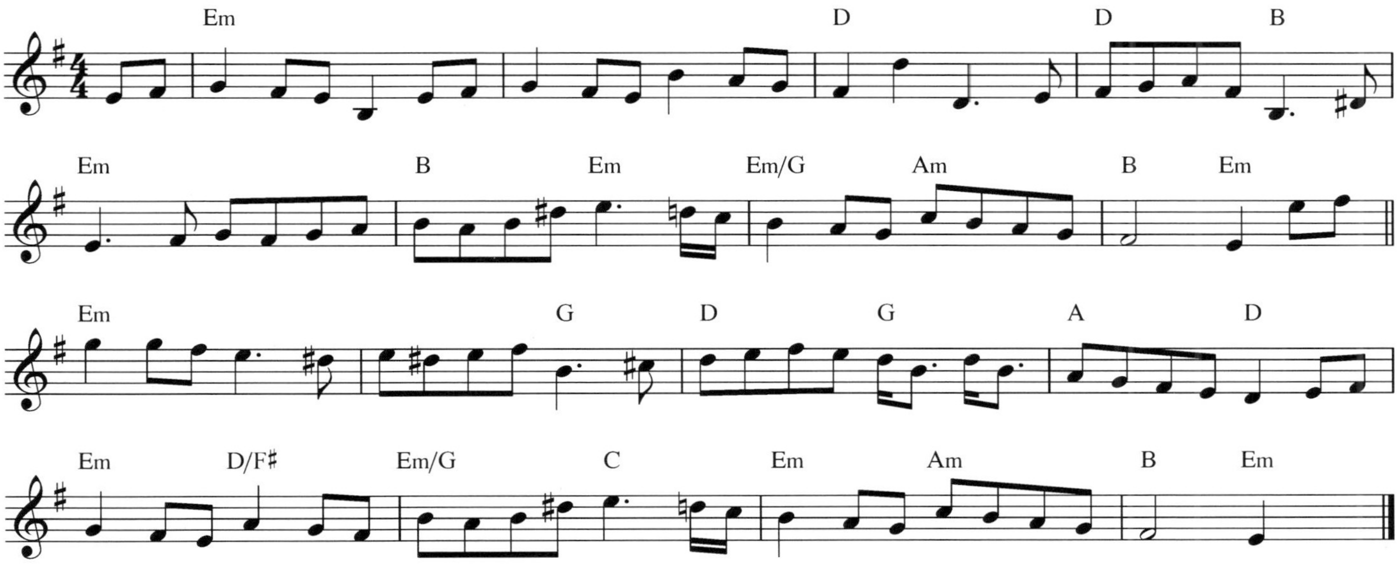

The melody for this poignant song strathspey is the tune "My love is lost to me." Robert Burns set his poem, "O Were I on Parnassus Hill" to it, and included it in Volume 3 of *The Scots Musical Museum*.

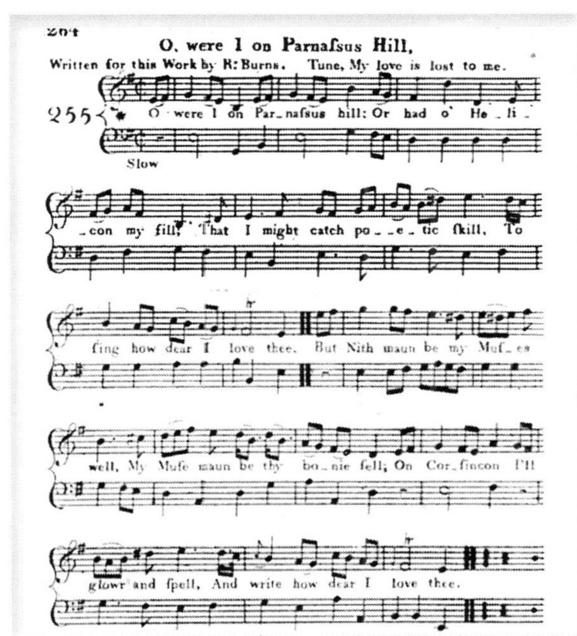

Mary Morrison

F major

Song by Robert Burns; tune is "The Miller" (traditional)

This is another lovely song strathspey, in the same genre as "O Were I On Parnassus Hill" and "The Mill Mill O." Like "Parnassus Hill," the title is also from a Robert Burns poem. We don't really know who Mary Morrison was. She may have been the Mary Morrison who is buried in a graveyard in Mauchline, and who was acquainted with Burns, but as he only met her once, and she would have been about 14, it is unlikely. According to the *Burns Encyclopedia* (www.robertburns.org), it is more likely that the real Mary Morrison was in fact a young lady named Alison Begbie, who was courted by Burns.

Burns wrote the poem in about 1784, and he planned to set it to a tune called "Duncan Davidson." Between 1784 and 1818, the poem appeared with two or three different melodies. Since then it has usually been paired with this tune, "The Miller," an old melody which was included in James Johnson's collection, *The Scots Musical Museum* (6 volumes printed from 1787–1803).

Tibby Fouller

G minor

Traditional

"Tibby Fouller o' the Glen" is an old melody, various versions in different keys appearing in early 18th-century tune books. It was printed in *Anderson's Budget of Strathspeys, Reels, and Country Dances for the German Flute or Violin* in 1820. It appears in at least two other versions, one included in John Glen's collection (in G minor), and one in Alexander MacGlashan's 1780 collection (in D minor).

Besides being a strathspey, "Tibby Fouller" (or "Fowler") is a song—a story of a beautiful young woman who was left a large sum of money by her parents; tired of all the false lovers who wanted to marry her for her money, she vowed she would marry only the man who would love her for herself. You can read the whole narrative, colorfully told, in *Wilson's Tales of the Borders and of Scotland*, by John Mackay Wilson (1857). (http://www.electricscotland.com/bordertales/vol1story2.htm)

Lord Byron's

E minor

Traditional

The poet Lord Byron (George Gordon) spent the early part of his short, tumultuous life in Scotland. He was the son of a rather disreputable English father, Capt. John ("Mad Jack") Byron, and a Scottish mother, Catherine Gordon of Gight. When "Mad Jack" abandoned them, young Catherine and two-year-old George, who was born with a deformed foot and needed medical care, moved back to Catherine's native Aberdeen. Lord Byron lived there until he was 10, when he inherited Newstead Abbey, in Nottinghamshire, from his great-uncle, and left Scotland.

Another lovely tune, not a strathspey, but a reel, called "Miss Gordon of Gight," was composed for Lord Byron's mother, Catherine (Byron) Gordon, by Isaac Cooper in about 1790. Catherine was descended from royalty (James I of Scotland) on the Gordon side of her family. Despite this noble lineage, she was unfortunately known for being hot-tempered, unattractive, and not well-educated. She made sure, however, that her son did receive an excellent education, and took good care of him. Byron's literary abilities showed themselves early as he took on the duties of writing letters for her by the age of ten.

Rob Roy MacGregor

E minor

Traditional

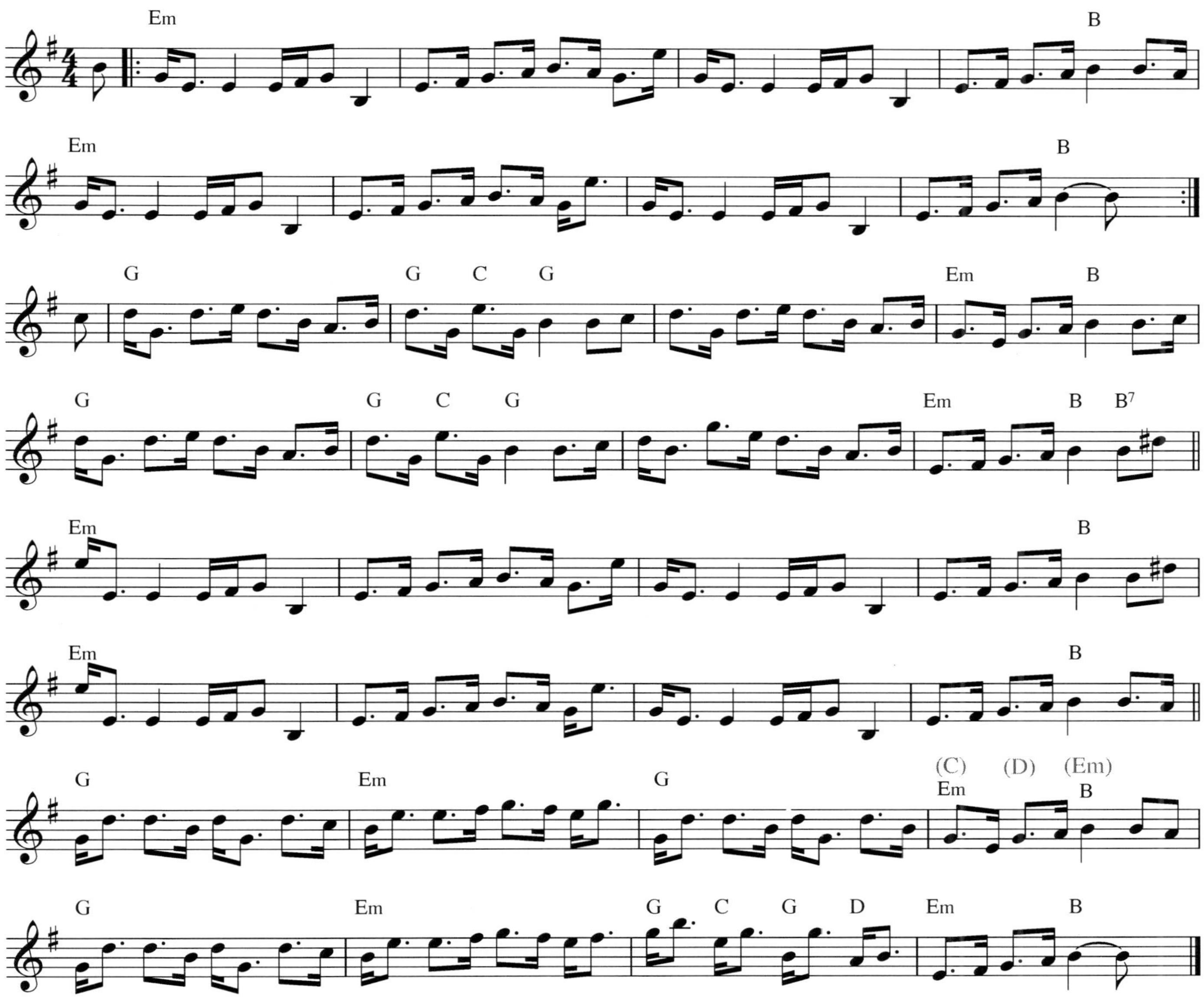

Legends surround Rob Roy MacGregor's name. A kind of Highlands Robin Hood, he was born about 1660. Through a misfortunate chain of events, he was reduced from landed gentleman to outlaw, waging a long-term war with the Duke of Montrose, who had confiscated all his lands and property for failure to repay debts on time. Rob Roy's Cave, one of his hiding places, overlooks Loch Lomond, near Inversnaid.

A strong, powerful strathspey, to be played with bravado!

Gorthleck's Highland Plaid

E major

Anonymous

Captain Simon Fraser included "Gorthleck's Highland Plaid" in an appendix to his *Airs and Melodies Peculiar to the Highlands of Scotland and the Isles* (1816), with a story about how it came to be written. Fraser's grandfather, Thomas Fraser, Esq., of Gorthleck, offered hospitality to many people during the time of the 1745 Rebellion. Lord Lovat and his "attendant Minstrel and Bard," were staying at the house, and on one of the occasions when the bard was playing music for the company, "Old Gorthleck" (Thomas Fraser) appeared wearing a beautiful new belted plaid. The bard complimented him on it, whereupon Gorthleck granted him the old one he had been wearing—a very generous gift! The bard immediately commemorated the occasion by composing this tune and playing it for Gorthleck and his visitors.

Belted Plaid

Miss Jessie Smith

D major

Traditional

Last time, resolve on D chord

This tune is a favorite among Scottish musicians. It appeared in Book 4 of Joseph Lowe's six-volume *Collection of Reels, Strathspeys & Jigs* (1844–45). Who Miss Jessie Smith was, we do not know, but this strathspey is a wonderful dance tune, with much motion and energy.

Cock of the North

Bb major

Traditional

The "Cock of the North" is the nickname given to the chief of the Gordon Clan, the Duke of Gordon. The Gordons' holdings were vast, stretching across much of north-east Scotland, including Huntly Castle, Auchindoun Castle, Fyvie Castle, Haddo House, and Gordon Castle.

Another nickname for the Gordon Clan chief is "Gudeman of the Bog," from the Bog of Gight, the site of Gordon Castle, near Fochabers.

This tune, of course, is a strathspey; there is a different tune, a 6/8 march with the same title, which is the Gordon Clan march.

This version of the tune is from Capt. Simon Fraser's 1816 collection, *The Airs and Melodies Peculiar to the Highlands of Scotland and the Isles*. It's a tough and gritty tune, and, for fiddlers, not particularly easy to play. It demands a lot of bow, and a lot of spunk and conviction!

The Gordon Clan crest

Brechin Castle

Bb major

Traditional

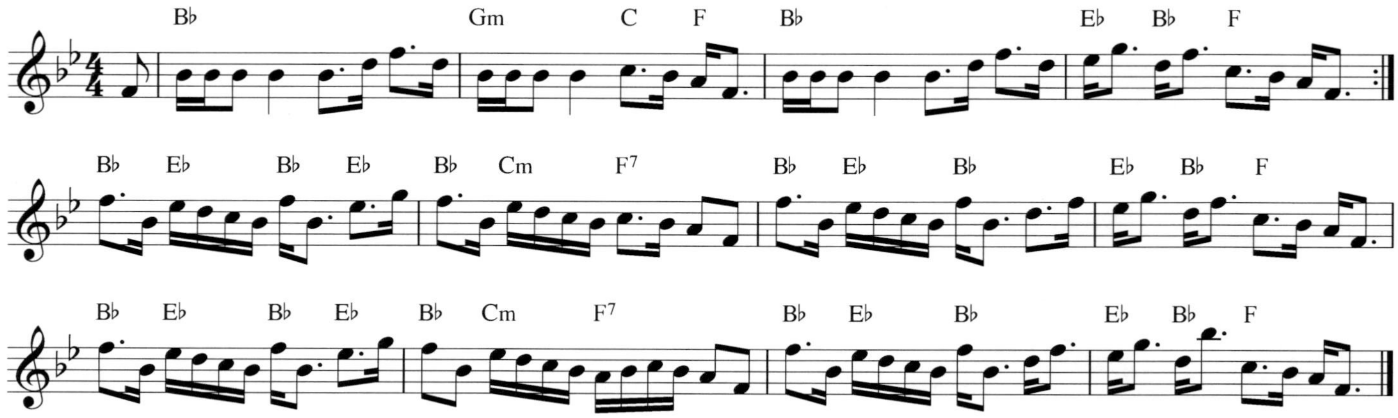

Last time: resolve to Bb
on a final bow chord

Brechin Castle has had a long and venerable history. The castle as it stands today was largely rebuilt in the 18th century, but the vast estate holdings have been in the Maule (of Panmure) and Ramsay (of Dalhousie) families since the 13th century. Lord and Lady Dalhousie now reside there, and the castle and extensive grounds are open to visitors.

The Bridge of Brechin, near Brechin Castle

Bridge of Brechin

F major

Joseph Lowe, 1797–1866

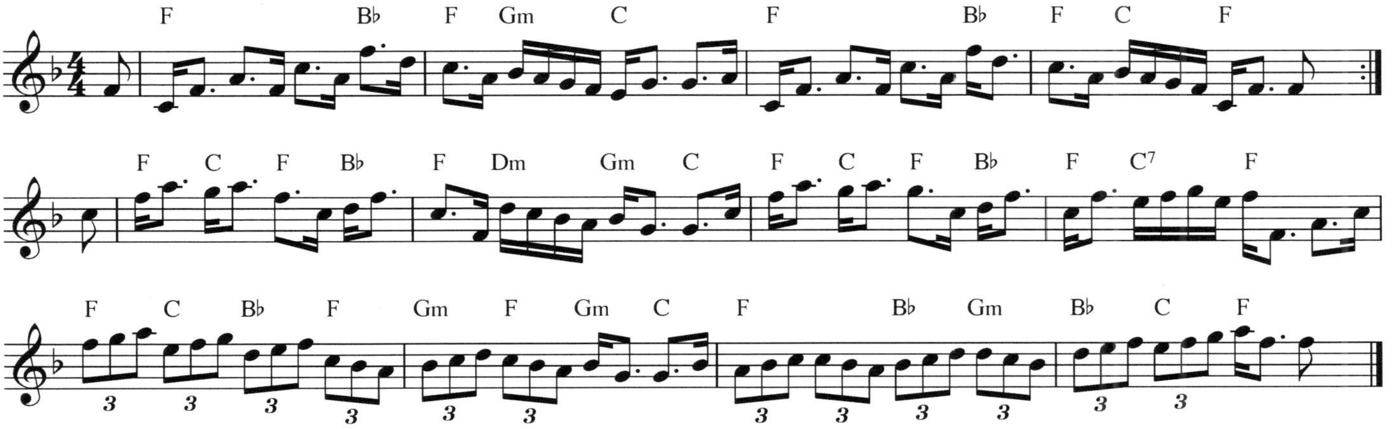

Joseph Lowe was a dancing-master to Queen Victoria and her children, and accompanied the royal family on their travels to Balmoral Castle and Windsor Castle in the 1850s. He kept a diary of his experiences teaching the family quadrilles, reels, and all the dances in fashion during that time. He would play his fiddle while teaching, as most dancing-masters did.

Marykirk town gate. Joseph Lowe's father lived in this town, not far from Brechin.

The Lowes were a musical family. Joseph's father, John Lowe, was a dancing-master in the town of Marykirk, and also a fine fiddle player and composer. He wrote the well-known reel, "Rachael Rae." Joseph's brothers, Robert and John Lowe, were also dancing-masters and composers. Joseph was apprenticed to a saddler as a young man, but as his musical talent began to tug him in other directions, he joined his brother Robert in Brechin, teaching dancing and music. He later moved on to Inverness, where he was a violin teacher.

"The Bridge of Brechin" is one of Lowe's compositions that he included in the sixth volume (1845) of *Lowe's Collection of Reels, Strathspeys and Jigs, being a new and complete selection of the dancing tunes in their proper keys, as performed at the different assemblies and public meetings throughout Scotland.* Interesting that the dancing-master is concerned about the key the tunes are in…

Avimore

A major

Joseph Lowe, c. 1797–1866

Aviemore is a small town in the heart of the Cairngorm Mountains, along the river Spey. Its wild and mountainous location still makes it a popular retreat for hikers, skiiers, and naturalists. It is across the Spey River from the village of Rothiemurchus, and within a few miles of Carrbridge, where the skeleton of the Old Packhorse Bridge still stands.

The Old Packhorse Bridge was supposed to be a solution to the problem of how to cross the River Dulnain when it was in spate. In the early 18th century, there was no place to cross it, and burials at the local church in Duthil often had to be delayed until the river subsided.

Alexander Grant of Grant commissioned a new bridge to be built, and in November 1717, the Packhorse Bridge was completed.

Floods and weather took their toll, however. The parapets and side walls were badly damaged during the later part of the 18th century, and again in a flood in August 1829, leaving the bridge looking as it does today.

Mrs. McInroy of Lude

B minor

Joseph Lowe, c. 1797–1866

On a very rural, wooded hillside not far from Blair Atholl and Blair Castle, in Perthshire, stands Lude House, the seat of the McInroys. The McInroys bought the Lude estate from the Robertsons in 1818, and consequently became well-established in Atholl. Lude is at the southern end of the Cairngorm Mountains.

Joseph Lowe, who composed this beautiful, strong, and lyrical strathspey, lived in Marykirk, in Perthshire. As dancing-master to the royal family for a number of years, and as a well-respected musician, he would probably have had many opportunities to meet visitors, perhaps the McInroys, who might have been invited to Balmoral Castle, not far distant from Lude.

About five miles away from Lude, on the River Tay, is Dunkeld, where Beatrix Potter often stayed as a child on summer holidays, and from where her inspiration for the Peter Rabbit stories came.

Monymusk
(Sir Archibald Grant of Monemusk's)
A major

Daniel Dow, 1732–1783

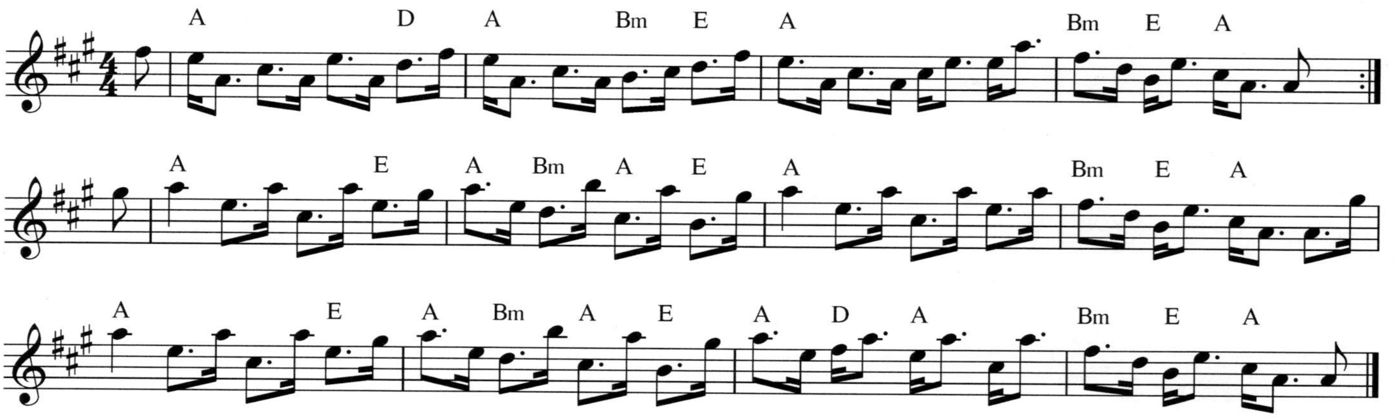

This famous tune has traveled from its native Scotland to America, morphed from strathspey to reel, changed keys, and added variations and parts in its 225-year history. It's just a great tune, whether it's a Scottish strathspey or an old-time reel. Many Scottish fiddlers prefer it in the key of A, as it lies well on the fiddle that way, but it has appeared in many collections in G major and other keys.

A doorway in Monymusk

Sir Archibald Grant of Monemusk (1696–1778) was an agricultural reformer who took ownership of and completely transformed the village of Monymusk, in Aberdeenshire, draining the land and improving farming techniques. Today it is a charming village with a church, a town square, a hotel and post office, and numerous small houses surrounding the square.

Daniel Dow (or Donald Dow, as he was also known) lived in Edinburgh for much of his life. He was admired as an excellent composer, and was a popular music teacher, particularly of violin and guitar. He published several collections of tunes during his short life (he died of fever when he was only 51). John Glen, in a biographical note about Dow, writes, "It is important to observe that Nathaniel Gow and others, changed the names of several of Dow's tunes, when including them in their own collections."

Miss Urquhart of Meldrum

D major

Isaac Cooper, 1755–1820

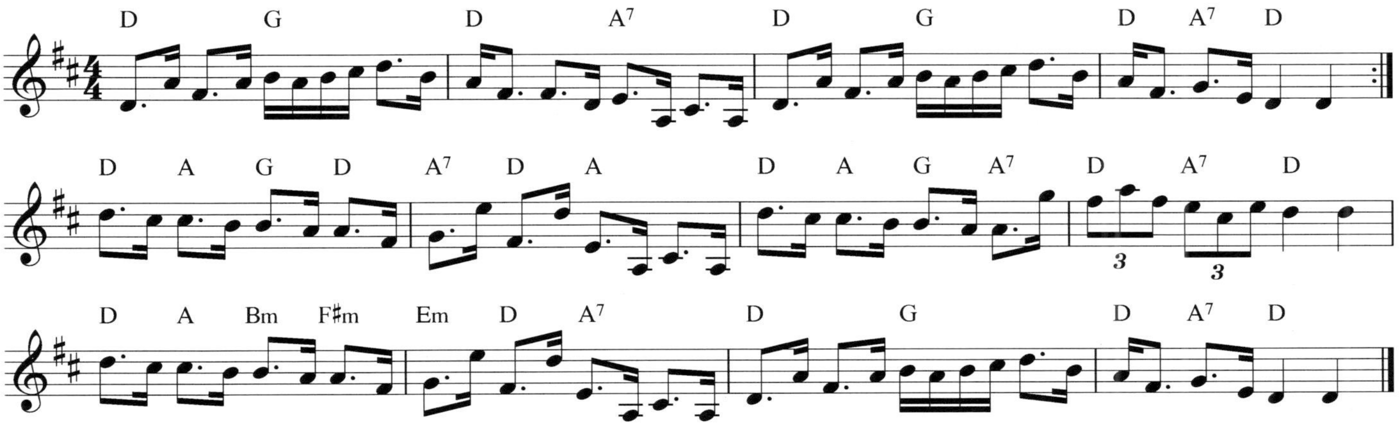

Isaac Cooper did not compose large volumes of music, but what he did write always seems to be very musical and well-constructed. David Baptie, in his book, *Musical Scotland, Past and Present* (1894) says that Cooper was known as "an excellent composer of dance music, and an able teacher." He lived in Edinburgh for much of his life, but began and ended his life in Banff, dying "in very indigent circumstances," as Baptie said, adding, "so soon does fame pass away." As a teacher in Edinburgh, Cooper was tremendously popular, and was able not only to give lessons in many instruments, but in dancing as well.

Many of Cooper's tunes are associated with the town of Banff: "Banff Castle," "Lord Banff," "Duff House," and his well-known melody, "Miss Forbes' Farewell to Banff." In 1788, Miss Forbes married James Urquhart of Meldrum, a town not far from Banff. Cooper would have been acquainted with the Urquharts, whose family seat in that area was at Meldrum, and who also had close family ties with the Gordons.

Georgian Building on Site of Royal Medieval Castle – Banff –

Cooper published two collections of tunes, many of them his own, in 1783, and in 1806. This strathspey was in both collections, but when it appeared in the 1806 collection, it had been renamed "Miss Gordon of Nethermuir."

Lord Banff's

E major

Isaac Cooper, 1755–1811

This lovely, rather sweet, E major strathspey must have been one that Isaac Cooper was proud of. This version appears in his first collection, where he calls it "Lord Banff's Reel." It also appears in his second collection, as "Lord Banff's – Dancing Sett," and he has put it in D major instead. Another version of it appears a few pages later, as "Lord Banff's Strathspey," in E major, as a four-part tune with a challenging series of variations. Cooper noted that this four-part version should be played slowly; it was most likely intended to be a concert or performance piece.

The title, "Lord Banff," belonged to the Ogilvy family. Cooper published this tune for the first time in 1783, when Sir William Ogilvy held the title. By the time Cooper published his second collection, in 1806, Sir William had died, with no heirs, and the title of Lord Banff became extinct.

Mrs. James Duff's Strathspey

A major

Isaac Cooper, 1755–1811

Duff House is a grand 18th-century estate just on the outskirts of Banff, the town where Isaac Cooper lived for much of his life. Close to the Banff harbor and the River Deveron, the house was built in the 1730s for the Duff family; today it is open to the public as part of the National Gallery of Scotland.

Duff House, Banff

Eglinton Castle

Bb major

Attributed to Hugh Montgomery, Earl of Eglinton, 1739–1819

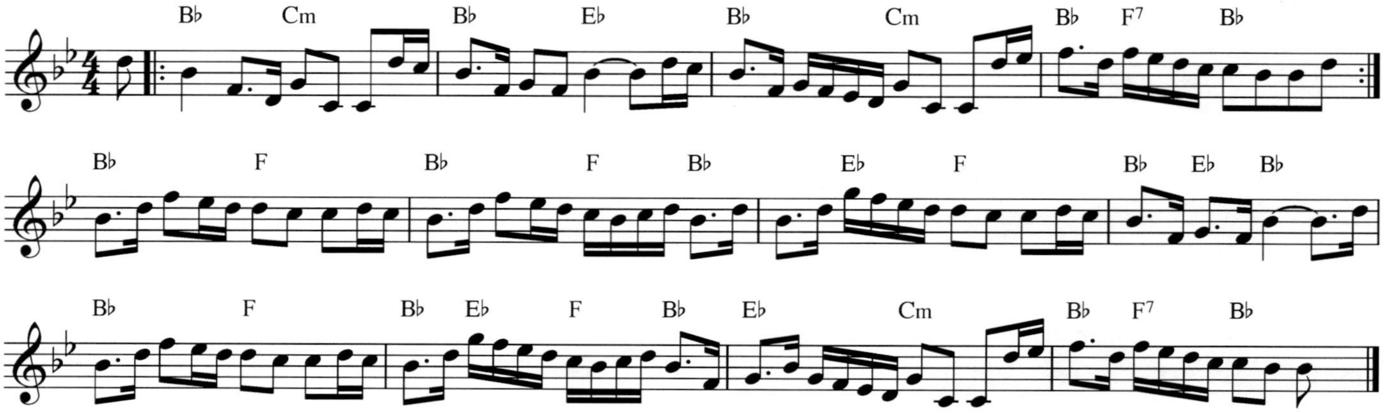

Hugh Montgomery (or Montgomerie, another common spelling), 12th Earl of Eglinton, was from Coilsfield, Ayrshire. Besides being a Member of Parliament, a military officer, and a career politician, he was a cellist and composer. He published a set of three duets for flutes or violins anonymously in about 1775, a set of *New Strathspey Reels* in 1796, and wrote several songs. John Riddell, a well-known Scottish fiddler and composer, wrote the beautiful slow air "Coilsfield House" in his honor. John Singleton Copley painted a heroic portrait of him in 1780, after Montgomery's return from fighting in the French and Indian War at Ticonderoga and the American War of Independence. The painting is owned by the Los Angeles County Museum of Art, in California.

Eglinton Castle, built by Hugh Montgomery in 1797, still remains, but only as a picturesque turreted ruin in Kilwinning, near Ardrossan and Glasgow.

This tune, probably composed about 1800, appears in the *Gow Collection of Scottish Dance Music* (#54), with the title "Earl of Eglinton." It is from the 4th collection of Niel Gow's reels, and appears as "Eglinton Castle." If played slowly, as the tempo marking in the Gow Collection indicates, that would allow the player to bring out more of the strathspey-like characteristics of the tune. This is a melody, however, that if played more quickly, takes on the personality of a march rather than a strathspey.

Lady Glasgow

A major

Hugh Montgomery, Earl of Eglinton, 1739–1819

Another of Hugh Montgomery's compositions, this one appears in Book II of John Glen's *Collection of Scottish Dance Music, Strathspeys, Reels, and Jigs*. This tune has much more of the personality of a strong strathspey than Montgomery's "Eglinton Castle."

Lady Glasgow may have been Lady Augusta Hay (1766–1822), who was married to Sir George Boyle, 4th Earl of Glasgow. She may have been distantly related to Hugh Montgomery by marriage.

Eglinton Castle ruins

Sir Alexander Don

G minor

Robert Mackintosh, 1745–1807

Sir Alexander Don (1751–1815) was an amateur composer himself (he composed a tune called "The Caledonian Hunt," and appreciated the musicians who graced Scotland's manor houses and balls. A sportsman and hunter, he and several other gentlemen created the Caledonian Hunt society, whose annual ball was a headliner event for the Scottish aristocracy. Nathaniel Gow was a regular performer at the ball for many years. In 1798, the Caledonian Hunt society presented Nathaniel Gow with a bonus payment of ten guineas, and they called him "their musician, the famous Nathaniel Gow"—high praise, by any measure! Sir Alexander even presented Nathaniel Gow with a valuable Italian violin, in admiration of his music.

Lady Brome's

C minor

Robert Mackintosh, 1745–1807

Lady Brome was Louisa, the fourth daughter of Alexander, Duke of Gordon, and his resilient wife, Jane Maxwell. Louisa married Viscount Brome, the oldest son of General Cornwallis, of American Revolutionary War fame.

This tune is another of "Red Rob" Mackintosh's powerful and dramatic strathspeys. As John Glen said, in his brief biographical sketches of major Scottish composers in 1891, "he was a musician of the first order in Scottish music."

Lady Louisa Gordon Cornwallis

Mrs. Adye (Mrs. Adie)

Bb major

William Logan, 1745–1819

Who Mrs. Adye (or Mrs. Adie) may have been remains a mystery—she was another 18th-century lady commemorated in a lovely tune. The composer, however, was Major William Logan of Camlarg, Ayrshire. He was a violinist, a composer, and a friend of Robert Burns, who immortalized him in a poem, "Epistle to Major Logan" (1786):

> Hail, thairm-inspirin', rattlin' Willie!
> Tho' fortune's road be rough an' hilly
> To every fiddling, rhyming billie,
> We never heed,
> But take it like the unback'd filly,
> Proud o' her speed.
> …
> Hale be your heart! hale be your fiddle!
> Lang may your elbuck jink and diddle,
> To cheer you through the weary widdle
> O' this wild warl'.
> Until you on a crummock driddle,
> A grey hair'd carl.

"Thairm" means "guts," or "intestines"; fiddle strings would have been made of gut, and an excellent fiddler would be quite capable of "inspiring" the strings.

The Duke of Gordon's Birthday

G major

William Marshall, 1748–1833

This grand and cheerful strathspey was one of the earliest tunes that Marshall composed after he began working at the Gordon Castle estate as butler and house-steward. The Gordons openly appreciated his musical abilities, and encouraged him to write and play tunes for many occasions and guests. He was probably as close as anyone could be to being a part of the family.

Even after Marshall retired from the service of the Gordons, in 1817, the family came to visit him frequently, and invited him to the Castle on many occasions. George, the Marquis of Huntly who became Duke of Gordon after his father passed the title on to him, requested Marshall to sit for his portrait with John Moir—the famous painting of Marshall sitting, looking kindly, holding his violin as if about to pick it up to play. Marshall was seventy years old when the portrait was made.

Sketch from the 1818 John Moir portrait of Marshall

Marquis of Huntly

G minor

William Marshall, 1748–1833

This beautiful strathspey was another of William Marshall's early compositions, written about the same time as "The Duke of Gordon's Birthday," "The Bog of Gight," and "Miss Admiral Gordon."

Understanding titles of the Scottish aristocracy can be a little challenging, at the very least, to those not "to the manor born." Although not born into the aristocracy, Marshall would have been quite comfortable with the conventions. He was employed by the Duke of Gordon for thirty years, first as a butler and steward, and after 1790, as a factor, or manager, of the Gordon estate. He grew up with and knew the family well. The title Marquis (occasionally written as Marquess) of Huntly, in Aberdeenshire, was the secondary title of the Duke of Gordon. The title of Marquis was usually given to a first-born son.

The Marquis of Huntly honored by this beautiful strathspey was George, the oldest son of the Duke, born in 1770. He was the same Marquis for whom Marshall wrote "The Marquis of Huntly's Farewell." All the members of the Gordon family seem to have been fond of music and dance; the halls of Gordon Castle must have resonated with the sounds of fiddle and cello.

Marquis of Huntly's Farewell

A major

William Marshall, 1748–1833

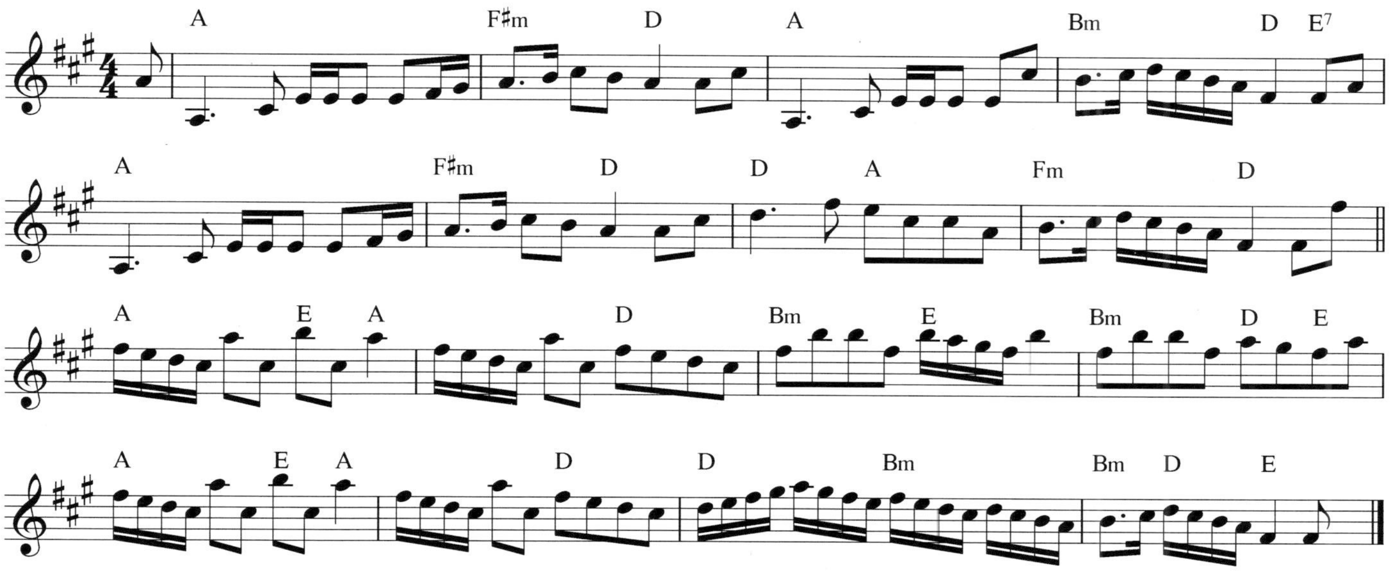

Last time: resolve to A
on a final bow chord

This beautiful, strong strathspey is one of William Marshall's champion compositions. The story behind it is that he wrote it, reflecting on the departure of the young Marquis of Huntly from Gordon Castle on his first journey abroad:

> ...a very tender scene took place at the castle. The elder branches embraced him and expressed their grief in tears and murmurings. The younger children clung to their brother's knees and arms, and in sharper notes gave vent to their feelings. Marshall was present during this scene, and taking up his violin, immediately produced his beautiful air...he endeavoured in the first part to imitate the wailing of the parents, and in the latter bars that of his young sisters.
>
> From "Memoir of William Marshall, Composer," by Joseph MacGregor (1845)

Miss McQueen

F major

William Marshall, 1748–1833

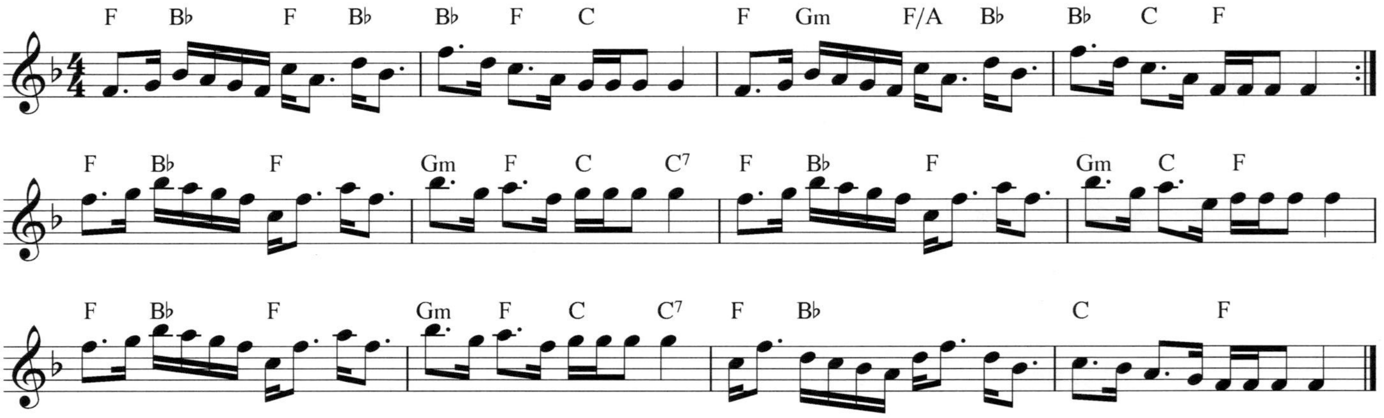

This strathspey appeared in William Marshall's collection of 36 tunes published in 1781. Over the course of his life, he wrote more than 250 tunes, many in honor of friends and associates of the Gordon family. Unfortunately, most of the people whose names are immortalized in tunes have only the tunes to commemorate them. The Miss McQueen of this strathspey may have lived at Strathdown, in Banffshire.

Along the main street in Banff

Miss Admiral Gordon

A major

William Marshall, 1748–1833

O a' the airts the wind can blaw,
I dearly lo'e the west
For there the bonnie lassie lives,
The lass that I lo'e best.
Tho' wild woods grow an' rivers tow,
Wi' mony a hill between,
Baith day and nicht, my fancy's flicht,
Is ever wi' my Jean.

Gordon Castle

For anyone familiar with the songs of Robert Burns, this strathspey will immediately be recognized as "Of a' the airts the wind can blaw," which Burns wrote for his wife-to-be, Jean Armour.

Burns may have met William Marshall when Burns was on a Highlands tour in 1787, and he dined with the Duke of Gordon at Gordon Castle, where Marshall was employed. He knew Marshall's reputation as a fine musician and composer, and he described him as "the first composer of strathspeys of the age," with a strong gift for melody.

Marshall wrote this strathspey in about 1775, in honor of Margaret Gordon, the only surviving child of Admiral William Gordon (d. 1769), of Banff; Gordon's four other children had died before they reached adulthood.

Banks o' Spey

A minor

William Marshall, 1748–1833

Craigellachie Bridge over the River Spey

"Strath" means valley; the valley of the river Spey is the birthplace of the type of tune and dance called a strathspey. The fastest-running river in Scotland, and the second-longest, the Spey does not waste time meandering, but springs headlong from out of the Scottish highlands, straight into the Moray Firth in the northeast part of Scotland. Whisky distilleries abound in this Speyside region.

You might hear someone say "The Spey is in spate"—not a good time to float peacefully down the river! This means the river is in flood, and on a number of occasions it has broken through its earthen embankments and carried away portions of towns, roads, and golf courses along its banks, including parts of the walls surrounding Gordon Castle, where William Marshall worked and lived. This beautiful, expressive tune captures the strength and emotional power of the River Spey.

The Forest of Ga-ick

D minor

William Marshall, 1748–1833

The Forest of Ga-ick, or Gaick, is a wild, remote, mountainous area south of Inverness and west of the Cairngorms. Its reputation as a dangerous place is probably warranted, as it is prone to avalanches, and a number of hunters and hikers have died there. A monument stands in a spot not far from the Gaick Lodge, near the Duke of Gordon's Well, marking a spot where five hunters were buried in an avalanche in January, 1800. Superstitions abound—tales of whirlwinds, demonic encounters, hauntings—but whatever the cause of the accident, the Forest of Gaick gave William Marshall inspiration for a beautifully haunting, D minor strathspey.

Monument to the 1800 avalanche

Croughly

D minor

William Marshall, 1748–1833

Croughly (pronounced approximately as "creek-ly"with the "k" aspirated, like "loch") is a farmhouse in Ballindalloch, Scotland, overlooking the rugged and beautiful Cairngorm Mountains. The original cottage was built around 1560, and was added onto in 1760. Today, it is a bed and breakfast as well as a farm, and not far from the famed Glenlivet distillery, which is reputed to have begun at Croughly Cottage as an illicit still.

Willliam Marshall lived not far distant from Croughly Cottage, and wrote in one of his many letters that he had a great fondness for "old Croughly." Croughly was part of the Gordon lands.

On the road in the Cairngorm Mountains

Mrs. Hugh Lumsden of Pitcaple

A major

William Marshall, 1748–1833

Mrs. Hugh Lumsden was Frances Brebner, who married Hugh Lumsden, Esq. in 1813, in Aberdeen. They had one daughter, Christina. Frances and her family would have been well known to William Marshall.

Pitcaple Castle, where the Lumsden family lived, is in Inverurie, not far from Aberdeen. The castle dates from the 15th century, and has its share of legends and hauntings. It was visited by King James IV in 1511, by Queen Mary in 1562, and by Charles II in 1650. Today, it is the residence of the Burgess - Lumsden family.

Frances Brebner (Mrs. Hugh Lumsden) died in 1815, only two years after her marriage, which may have inspired Marshall to compose this regal, graceful strathspey in her honor. A stone inscription in the Cathedral in Aberdeen commemorates the death of Frances, and of four of her siblings, all of whom died between 1815 and 1820.

Pitcaple Castle

The Bog of Gight

A major

William Marshall, 1748–1833

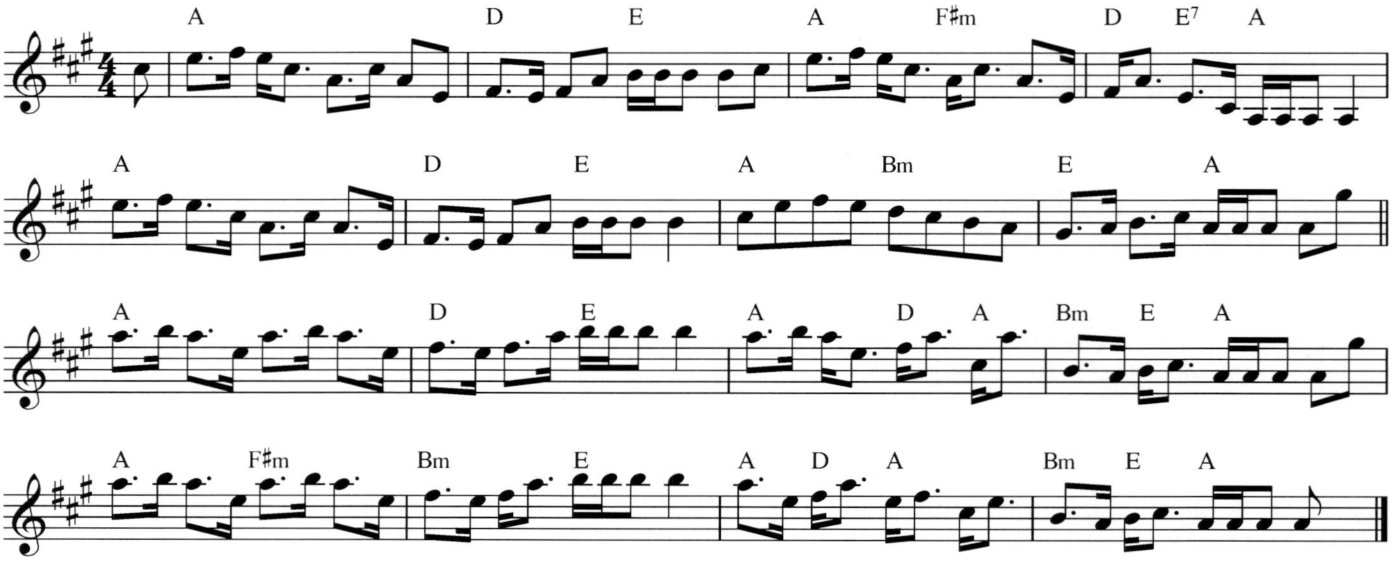

The Bog of Gight was synonymous with Gordon Castle—it is the name of the five-story medieval tower at the heart of the castle, and the land it was built on. As the estate factor, or manager, William Marshall was well familiar with the grounds of Gordon Castle, and he wrote many tunes centered around his life there.

The pond alongside Gordon Castle; there is a lovely walk beneath huge overhanging trees.

Keithmore

Eb major

William Marshall, 1748–1833

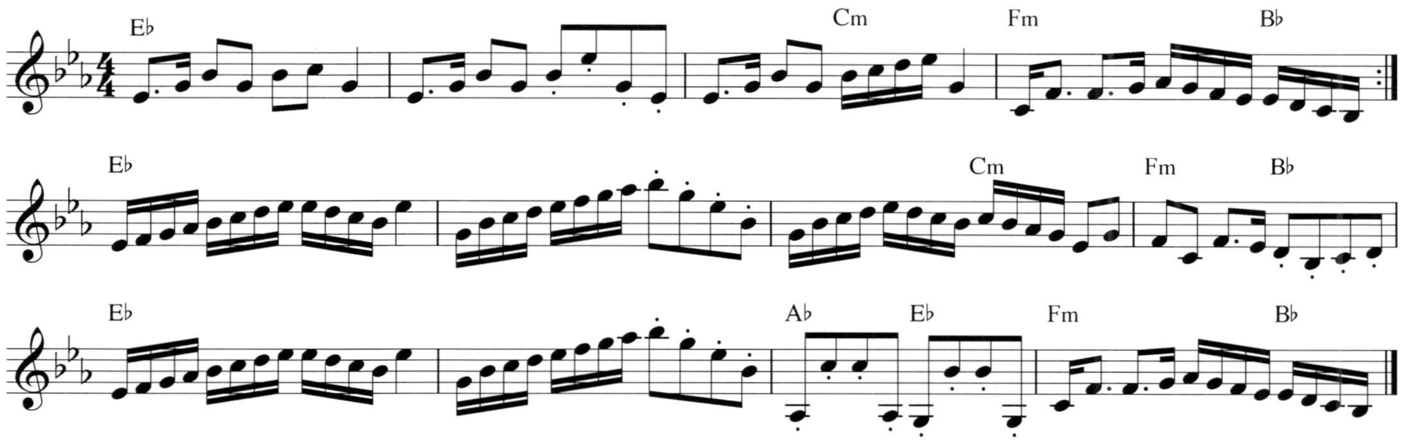

Last time: resolve to Eb on a final bow chord

Keithmore was William Marshall's farm, where he lived from about 1790 until he retired from the Duke of Gordon's service in 1817. The land was part of the Duke's properties, and Marshall very much enjoyed farming, and living at Keithmore. He had lived on and cultivated a small farm near Fochabers, not far from Gordon Castle. Keithmore was a larger farm, and Marshall must have taken much pleasure in having such a piece of land for his own.

Marshall's interests ranged widely—mathematics, clock-making, astronomy, optics, architecture, farming, surveying, falconry, hunting, athletics, and, of course, dancing. He was known as a "capital dancer," and this, no doubt, contributed to his ability to play so well that, as Joseph MacGregor wrote in his "Memoir of William Marshall, Composer" in 1845, "when he played reels or strathspeys, the inclination to dance on the part of old and young became irresistible." He was fond of musical scales outside the usual reach of folk fiddlers; he wrote many tunes in flat keys; and had no problem with notes on the fingerboard that required shifting out of first position.

And then, for us fiddle-players who discover that practice is the secret of excellent playing, there is the anecdote about Marshall's response to being criticized about the demanding nature of his pieces for fiddlers. He simply replied that he did not compose for "bunglers."

Back to the practice routine…

Kinrara

Bb major

William Marshall, 1748–1833

Marshall composed and published this beautiful air in 1800; he published it as a strathspey in 1822. He put a note in the 1822 collection: "This Strathspey was Composed by Mr. Marshall for the Duchess of Gordon, but is Published by Mr. Gow in his 4th Book, where he has changed its name, and called it the Countess of Dalkeith."

Kinrara was the home of Jane Maxwell, wife of Alexander, the 4th Duke of Gordon. Jane was beautiful, brilliant, a social flame, and highly determined. Her life reads like a novel.

She was born in 1749. Her family was respectable, related to the Earl of Eglinton, and owned land, although her father may not have been a stellar financial strategist. Nonetheless, Jane was educated in Edinburgh, took singing and drawing lessons, read and discussed literature with visiting writers and thinkers, and became an excellent dancer. She fell in love at 16, with a young officer, a Fraser, and a relative of Lord Lovat. Soon after they met, he left with his regiment to go to America, and some time later she received news that he had died.

Jane married the following year, to Alexander Gordon. He was wealthy and titled, a good marriage choice for her. While on their honeymoon in Berwickshire, she received a note from her former love, who was quite alive, asking her to marry him. The story goes that she read the note and fainted.

She must have thrown herself into her new life with all the energy she could. For the next 20 years, the Duke and Duchess of Gordon lived at Gordon Castle (the "Bog of Gight") near Fochabers. Marshall would have been the house-steward and butler during those years. Jane organized parties, planted trees, took a great interest in farming, and always included dancing and music at their gatherings. She probably encouraged the strathspey as a dance form. Without question, she encouraged music and dance in the household.

They had six children in the next 15 years. The first son, George, the Marquis of Huntly, was born in 1770. At the same time, the Duke fathered an illegitimate son, also named George, by Mrs. Jean Christie. Jane seems to have taken this in stride: she referred to the two children as "my George" and "the Duke's George."

Over the next two decades, she raised their children, four daughters and two sons. She entertained poets, politicians, princes, and was well-loved and respected in society, even in London, where she apparently charmed King George III into allowing her to promote her Scottish heritage when it was not politically safe to do so. She was an ardent admirer and sponsor of Robert Burns. She was a shining star in society.

By 1799, however, her older son, George, had gone off to serve in the military, and her second son, Alexander, died at 23. She became sad and depressed, missing her sons. At about the same time, her husband moved his mistress, Mrs. Christie, into Gordon Castle, and built Jane a small house—Kinrara— on the River Spey. Jane lived at Kinrara for the next few years, as the Duke's estranged wife. She continued to entertain, and made sure her daughters made good matches. Her daughter Louisa was to be engaged to the son of General Cornwallis, who had just returned from America. It looked like the General would not approve of the match, mentioning fears of madness in the Gordon family. In a startling turn of events, Jane Maxwell put his fears to rest, announcing that there was not one drop of Gordon blood in daughter Louisa. The marriage was approved.

No one knows who Louisa's father was, but it is possible that it was Jane's former love, the captain.

In 1805, the Duke and Duchess formally ended their marriage. Jane was assured of a new house and financial security. Unfortunately, the Duke was in financial difficulties himself, and he was not able to keep up his payments to her. Jane became impoverished; with no home, she had to live where she could, and she became bitter and eccentric. She died in a hotel in Piccadilly, London in 1812, with her children at her side.

Jane Maxwell was buried at the old Celtic Chapel on the banks of the Spey, at Kinrara.

Marchioness of Cornwallis

Eb major

William Marshall, 1748–1833

The Marchioness of Cornwallis was Louisa, the 4th daughter of Alexander (Gordon), the 4th Duke of Gordon, and Jane Maxwell. She married the oldest son of General Cornwallis (the son's title would have been Viscount Brome), later to be the Marquis of Cornwallis. Louisa thereby became the Marchioness of Cornwallis. She would also be known as Lady Brome, and Robert Mackintosh wrote a strathspey in her honor by that title.

This beautiful, slow strathspey was considered by the Duke of Gordon to be one of Marshall's best melodies. The Duke would signal that it was time for the end of a concert by calling for this tune to be played.

The Marchioness of Huntly's Strathspey

Bb major

William Marshall, 1748–1833

Marshall marked this version of the strathspey, in Bb major, to be played slowly, as a performance piece.

The Marchioness of Huntly was Elizabeth Brodie (1794-1864), wife of George (1770–1836), Marquis of Huntly and the future 5th Duke of Gordon. Elizabeth was the daughter of a wealthy merchant named Alexander Brodie and his wife, Elizabeth Wemyss. When Marshall published his 1822 collection of tunes, he dedicated it to her.

Elizabeth Brodie is reputed to have been an accomplished musician, and was very fond of traditional Scottish music. She enthusiastically promoted Marshall's musical endeavors, and also the Gows', who dedicated their *Sixth Collection of Strathspey Reels* to her. She must have been well appreciated; there are many tunes written in her honor.

Fireplace at Huntly Castle, with portraits of the first Marquis of Huntly and his wife, about 1599.

The Marchioness of Huntly's Strathspey

A major

William Marshall, 1748–1833

Marshall indicated in the publication of "The Marchioness of Huntly's Strathspey" in Bb major, that it should be "slow." In his accompanying note to the Bb version, however, he wrote: "When danced, may be played in A three Sharps."

If this tune were played for a dance, of course, it would be at dance tempo, more quickly than the Bb version, and the fermata in bar 5 of the B part would be removed (I have omitted it here).

Huntly Castle tower

John French's Compliments to Mr. Nathaniel Gow

E♭ major

John French, 1753–1803

Not much is known of John French, except that he was a "Fiddler-Composer of Ayr," as he described himself in his *Collection of New Strathspeys, Reels etc dedicated to Mrs Boswell of Auchinleck.* The collection was published in 1803, posthumously, by Gow and Shepherd, Nathaniel Gow's music publishing company, "for behoof of Mr French's widow and children."

This is a graceful-feeling strathspey; in the French collection it is marked to be played "slow."

Mrs. Boswell of Auchinleck, to whom French dedicated the collection of tunes, was the wife of James Boswell. James Boswell accompanied Dr. Samuel Johnson as his secretary on their journey in 1773 to the Hebrides, and published *The Journal of a Tour to the Hebrides with Samuel Johnson* in 1785.

Miss Maule of Panmure

C major

Nathaniel Gow, 1763–1831

The Maules, Earls of Panmure and Dalhousie, were well established in the area of Forfarshire and Perth. The family had extensive estates, including Brechin Castle and Panmure House. William Ramsay Maule (1771–1852) was very likely the father of the Miss Maule of Panmure for whom several strathspeys were written by various composers.

William Ramsay Maule was spirited, hot-tempered, and a bundle of contradictions. He did much to support social causes, and was a staunch patron of artists, writers, and musicians, including Robert Petrie, Niel Gow, and Nathaniel Gow. He also had an uncontrollable temper at times, and was likely to pull unpredictable pranks that sometimes got him into trouble. Andrew Kuntz, in his 2005 article about Maule, "The King of the Patrons," writes of Maule's often adolescent behavior—urbane and profligate; comic and annoying, all at the same time. Maule's obituary notice (he died at Brechin Castle in 1832) states that he was "a remarkable man…of natural shrewdness…he drew attention to himself by systematic defiance of conventional decorums…he was unmeasured in his loves and hatreds." He was notorious for excesses. We don't know much about his family, but his wife must have been a saint.

Miss Maule

A major

Robert Mackintosh, 1745–1807

Both of these tunes, written for a daughter of William Ramsay Maule (but we don't know which daughter; he had five) are quite different, and interesting. Robert Mackintosh's strathspey feels brave and forward-moving; Nathaniel Gow's seems more delicate and introspective.

The Dalhousie Arch, at the entrance to the village of Edzell, near Brechin

Countess of Airly

G major

John Bowie, 1759–1815

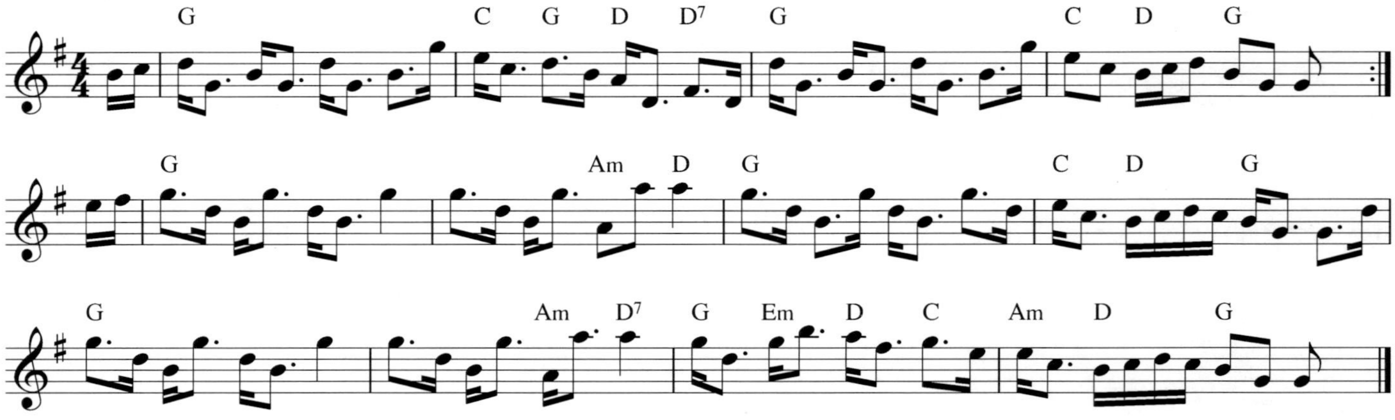

If you try playing this tune, you might see that it shares a bit of genetic material with "Monymusk." It was written by John Bowie, who was said to play delightfully on the fiddle, often accompanied by his brother, Peter, on bass. He published *A Collection of Strathspey Reels and Country Dances, &c*, in 1789, in Perth.

The Countess of Airly (or Airlie) was very likely one of the Ogilvy family, who have for 700 years lived in Airlie Castle and Cortachy Castle, near Kirriemuir. She must have been a strong person—this tune written in her honor is spiky and determined. For fiddle players, it is a great exercise in straddling two strings with one finger!

Captain Campbell of Carphen

A minor

Malcolm McDonald, fl. 1785–1800

This strathspey is well-known and loved. Its dark and rugged quality makes it a favorite among Scottish fiddlers. It is a dramatic tune, filled with snaps and ornamentation.

Almost nothing is known about Malcolm McDonald, who published four collections of tunes during his lifetime—one book of his own compositions, and three collections of other tunes. John Glen mentions that he resided in the Parish of Little Dunkeld, in Inver. We do know that he played cello with Niel Gow, after the death of Niel's brother, Donald Gow.

Fortingall Fairs

E minor

Malcolm McDonald, fl. 1785–1800

Fortingall is an beautiful, ancient village in Perthshire, with a history reaching back to Pictish origins. Roman ruins, a medieval chapel and large collection of medieval sculpture, a 5,000-year-old yew tree that may be the oldest on the planet, megalithic remains, and an array of Pictish standing stones grace this tiny town, not far from Loch Tay and Aberfeldy.

Fairs were often held several times a year in towns for the sale of seeds and livestock, and sometmes to celebrate the patron saint of the town.

Malcolm McDonald lived in Inver, not far from Fortingall.

Lady Burnside's Birthday

C minor

Charles Duff, c. 1760–1822

"Lady Burnside's Strathspey" was first published in Charles Duff's *Collection of Strathspeys, Reels, Jiggs &c with a Bass for the Violincello or Harpsichord* (c. 1790). Not a great deal is known about Charles Duff, who was a good musician "employed at concerts and balls," and who composed this somewhat driving, spiky tune. According to David Baptie, in his book, *Musical Scotland, Past and Present* (1894), Duff was a music teacher, born in Dundee, and was the "Duff" in the music-selling firm of Duff and Chalmers, about 1800. He may have been related to Archibald Duff, the dancing-master and composer from Montrose.

Lady Charlotte Bruce

A major

William Shepherd, 1760–1812

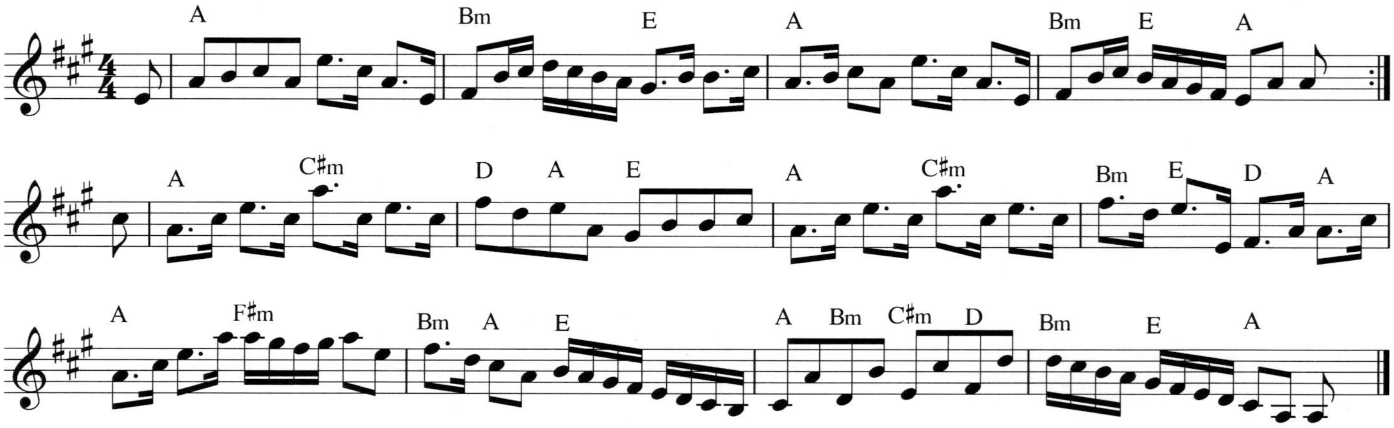

William Shepherd was Nathaniel Gow's business partner. Together they founded and operated Gow and Shepherd, Music Sellers, for many years, publishing numerous collections, including John Morison's, Malcolm McDonald's, and Niel Gow's. Nathaniel Gow continued the music publishing business after Shepherd died in 1812, despite financial difficulties, eventually changing the business name to Nathaniel Gow and Son.

This version of the tune is from Volume 2 of John Glen's *Collection of Scottish Dance Music.*

Lady Charlotte Matilda Bruce (1771–1816) was the third daughter of Charles, the 5th Earl of Elgin and Kincardine, and sister to Thomas, 7th Lord of Elgin. Lady Charlotte's brother, Thomas, Lord Elgin, earned much notoriety for gathering what would be called the Elgin Marbles—a large collection of statues, architectural specimens, artwork, and other treasures—from the Parthenon at Athens and bringing them back to England, where many of them now reside in the British Museum.

Lady Charlotte Campbell

G major

Nathaniel Gow, 1763–1831

Lady Charlotte Susan Maria Campbell (1775–1861) was famous for her great beauty. A portrait of her done in oils by Johann Tischbein hangs in the National Galleries of Scotland. However, besides being a beauty, and more befitting the idealized portrait of her, she was also a gifted musician, poet and novelist, a notion that was unfortunately not yet easily accepted in 18th-century Scottish society. She was well-loved for her sweet temperament and kindness. There are a number of tunes dedicated to her; Robert Mackintosh wrote a strathspey and a reel in her honor, and another tune with her name is also in the Gow collection. This one is written by Nathaniel Gow, son of Niel Gow.

Earl of Eglinton

E major

Nathaniel Gow, 1763–1831

This graceful, strong strathspey was composed by Nathaniel Gow in honor of Hugh Montgomery, the 12th Earl of Eglinton. The Earl was a cellist and a composer.

Miss Lucy Johnston's Compliments to Niel Gow

F major

Miss Lucy Johnston, 1765–1797

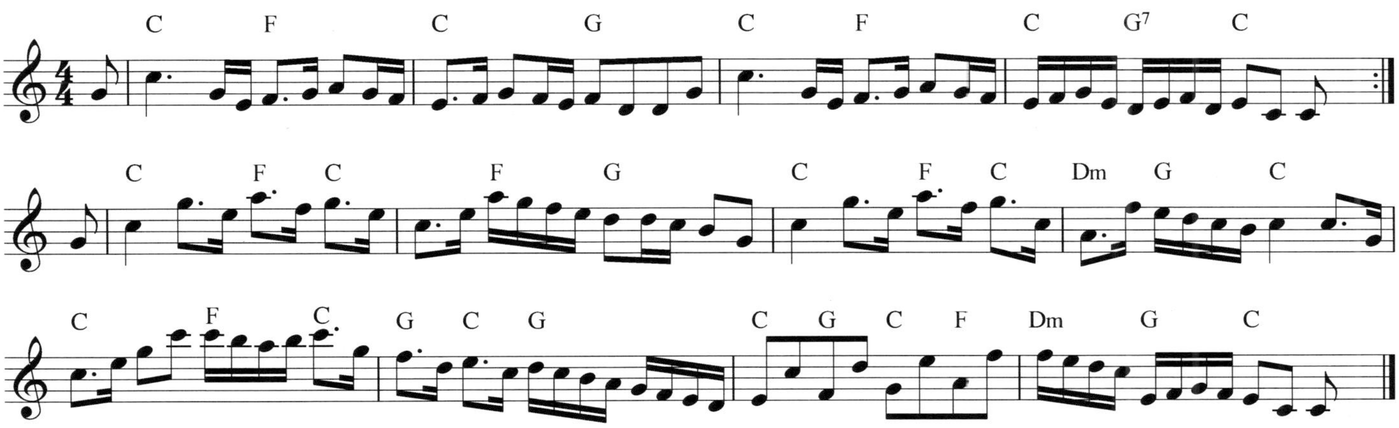

There are not many references to female composers in 18th-century Scotland, but there are a few. Miss Louisa (Lucy) Johnston of Hilton, by many accounts, was beautiful and well-known as a distinguished amateur musician and dancer. She was from an aristocratic family, one of six daughters in a family of eleven children. James Hunter, in *The Fiddle Music of Scotland* (1979), writes that she was a "noted belle of the Edinburgh Dance Assembly, … and was much admired by the Gows, Burns and Robert Mackintosh." Mackintosh dedicated his third collection of tunes to her; she was by that time Mrs. Oswald of Auchincruive. In 1799, Robert Burns notes her recent death of consumption in Lisbon, and dedicated the poem, "O Wat Ye Wha's in Yon Town," in her honor:

> …
> How blest ye birds that round her sing,
> And welcome in the blooming year,
> And doubly welcome be the spring,
> The season to my Lucy dear.
>
> The sun blinks blithe in yon town,
> And on yon bonnie braes of Ayr ;
> But my delight in yon town,
> And dearest bliss, is Lucy fair.

From *The Works of Robert Burns, Vol. 2,* edited by James Hogg and William Motherwell, Esq. (Glasgow,1834)

Wemyss Castle

Bb major

Robert Petrie, 1767–1830

Facing the salty gales of the Firth of Forth, across from Edinburgh, stands a 15th-century castle that was for centuries the seat of the Wemyss family, a strong force in Scottish history since the 12th century. Wemyss Castle is now a private residence, not open to the public, but the lovely Wemyss Castle Gardens are, including a beautiful six-acre walled garden dating from the 18th century.

Robert Petrie, who wrote this grand, imposing strathspey, was a fine violinist, teacher, and composer. He published four collections of dance tunes during his life, and was popular with the nobility, including the Hon. William Maule, Lord Panmure. He had another, rather reckless side, however; John Glen in his short biographical sketch of Petries says that he was thought of as a "ne'er-dae-weel" who got into more than his share of scrapes. He died in 1830 when he drowned in a stream, on the way home from a party. Regardless of his personal reputation, it is likely that Petrie would have been a welcome and frequent visitor at Wemyss Castle.

Pease Bridge

D minor

Abraham Mackintosh, 1769–c. 1810

In 1786, the world's highest bridge was the amazing four-arched Pease Bridge. It is 300 feet long, 16 feet wide, and 139 feet above ground. In its day it was something of a miracle, saving walkers a very long and dangerous descent and ascent through the chasm and across the burn, or stream, running through it. (Imagine the mail carrier having to struggle through this route, on horseback.)

The chasm that it crosses is the Pease Dean (originally Peathes), near Cockburnspath and Berwick-upon-Tweed, in the Scottish Borders region. Today, the Pease Dean and Tower Burn are part of a Scottish Wildlife Trust, and the easternmost part of the Southern Upland Way.

View of the Pease Bridge soon after it was built
(from *Antiquities of Scotland, Vol I*, by Francis Grose, pub. 1789)

Buckingham House
(Athole Brose)

D minor

Abraham Mackintosh 1769–c.1810

This is a dark, strong strathspey, written by Abraham Mackintosh, the son of Robert Mackintosh. It was printed in his father's collection, *Sixty eight New Reels and Strathspey's, Also above forty old Famous Reels for the Violin and Piano Forte* (1792). This same version was later printed in the John Glen *Collection of Scottish Dance Music*, Volume 2. In the R. Mackintosh collection, the composer's name is indicated: "by Mackintosh junior."

Although it is a strathspey, and is commonly played as a strathspey for dances, note that sometimes printers did not always notate the dotted eighths and sixteenths that give the strathspey its characteristic snaps. John Glen added "strathspey" next to the title in his collection; Mackintosh did not. Nonetheless, it would likely have been played with the snaps and feeling of a strathspey.

The alternate title, "Athole [or Atholl] Brose," refers to a potent brew made of oatmeal, water, and heather honey, stirred with a silver spoon. After a while, the liquid is strained out, and added to Scotch whisky. Legend says that the Duke of Atholl used it to capture his enemy, the Earl of Ross.

Buckingham House was the early name of what is now known as Buckingham Palace, which was being renovated in the late 18th century at great cost.

Crowhillock

A major

Archibald Duff, (c. 1770 – c. 1820 ?)

Crowhillock was a farm at Kinneff, owned by James Rae, the father of Rachel Rae. Rachel was immortalized in a well-known reel, a favorite among fiddlers today, composed by John Lowe (Joseph Lowe's father).

Like John Lowe, Archibald Duff, the composer of "Crowhillock," was a dancing-master. John Lowe was a dancing-master in Marykirk, near Kinneff; the tune, "Rachel Rae," was first printed in Archibald Duff's *Collection of Strathspeys, Reels, etc. for the pianoforte, violin and violincello* (1794). Duff's spirited, proud "Crowhillock" was published in this same volume.

North Side of the Grampians

C major

Capt. Simon Fraser, 1773–1852

This beautifully regal-sounding strathspey captures the feeling of the Grampians, the rugged mountain range which also includes the Cairngorms.

Fraser includes this in his *Collection of Airs and Melodies Peculiar to the Highlands of Scotland and the Isles* (1816), but does not claim it as his own composition. Joseph Lowe, however, does credit him with it, and says in a note below the tune that the tunes he has included by Capt. Fraser "are published by his special permission."

It seems a natural thing to pair this tune with James Porteous' "South of the Grampians," at least thematically, as the two tunes frame the Grampian mountain range. (Musically, they may need another tune between them that can transition gracefully.) James Porteous lived most of his life well south of the Grampians, in Ecclefechan, part of the Borders region near Dumfries and Annan. He was known and respected as a good violinist and composer; he published a collection of tunes in 1820. "South of the Grampians," originally called "Miss Rogerson's," was renamed "The Balance of Comfort," and was later given its current title.

South of the Grampians

A major

James Porteous, 1762–1847

South of The Grampians

Niel Gow's Style

B minor

Capt. Simon Fraser, 1773–1852

Last time: resolve to Bm
on a final bow chord

Simon Fraser probably included many tunes of his own in the *Collection of Airs and Melodies Peculiar to the Highlands of Scotland and the Isles*, and didn't credit himself with their composition. There were some, though, that he did quite clearly claim as his, and this is one of them. He notes that this strathspey "is merely Neil [Fraser's spelling] Gow's sprightly style imitated by the editor, in which his friends are pleased to say he has made a happy effort." It's a strong tune, well worth mastering the few technical challenges for fiddle players in the B part, too!

Northern Meeting

D major / B minor

Capt. Simon Fraser, 1773–1852

This angular-sounding strathspey (as published in Book 6 of Joseph Lowe's *Collection of Reels, Strathspeys & Jigs,* and noted as "by Capt. Fraser") conveys the sense of pride that families of the Northern Highlands must have felt as they gathered each autumn at the Northern Meeting. The rendezvous, begun in 1788 in Inverness, and still continuing, is now famous for the annual bagpipe competition. Jane Maxwell, the Duchess of Gordon during William Marshall's employment at Gordon Castle, was instrumental in organizing the Northern Meeting. Its original purpose was to "promote social intercourse" in the aftermath of the tragic events at Culloden in 1745, and to bring families together, no matter which side they had supported during the devastating 1745 rebellion.

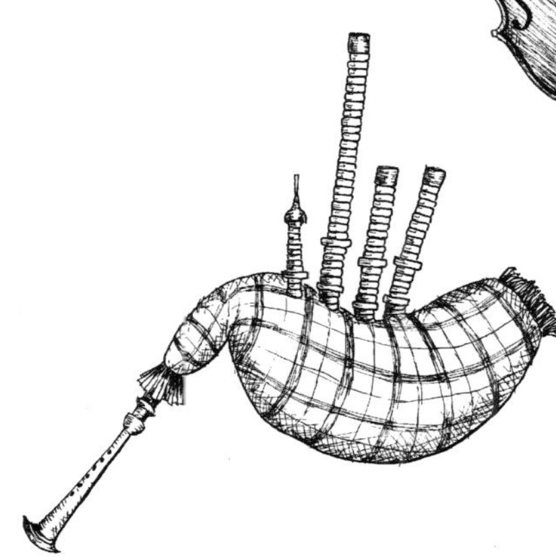

The Style of the Last Century

D minor

Capt. Simon Fraser, 1773–1852

Tunes in D minor seem to have a dark, gritty personality, and this is one of those! Written by Captain Simon Fraser, and included in his *Airs and Melodies Peculiar to the Highlands of Scotland and the Isles* (1816), he says modestly that it is "an attempt of the editor [Fraser] to imitate the style of the last century."

Braemar Castle

Huntly's Wedding Strathspey

A major

Capt. Simon Fraser, 1773–1852

This is one of Simon Fraser's tunes that he actually does take credit for. In the notes for the tune in his *Collection of Airs and Melodies Peculiar to the Highlands of Scotland and the Isles* (1816), he says that this strathspey and "Merry May the Pair Be," the reel that follows it in his collection, are intended as a medley honoring the wedding of the Marquis of Huntly. The wedding was celebrated not only at the Gordon castles, but throughout the Highlands, as families gathered at their own homes, lit bonfires on the tops of the hills, and danced to bagpipe and fiddle music. Huntly was well-loved and respected, and all wished to participate in wishing him well. Fraser calls him "an amiable nobleman," and modestly asks that his own "editor's mite" be permitted to commemorate the Huntly wedding. The "editor's mite" it may be, but it is a joyful and exuberant strathspey that can be played triumphantly!

Queen's Landing

B minor

Mr. Proudfoot

The key of B minor can be mysterious-sounding, and this tune feels like it has dark corners worth investigating. There is room for interpretation in this strathspey—it could be dark and foreboding, poignant, and powerful.

The identity of the composer, the mysterious Mr. Proudfoot, is not known; in fact, this may be the only strathspey composed by him that was printed. It appears in Joseph Lowe's *Collection of Reels, Strathspeys and Jigs*, in Volume 4.

As Joseph Lowe was the dancing-master for Queen Victoria and her family, and traveled with them back and forth from Balmoral to Windsor Castles, one wonders who "Mr Proudfoot" might have been—perhaps a dancing-master himself?

Dark Lochnagar

A major

Isabella Mary Scott (Gibson), 1786–1838

Lochnagar is a prominent, majestic mountain in the Cairngorms, overlooking Loch Muick, and easily visible from near Balmoral Castle and Braemar Castle, each only a few miles away.

This beautiful version of "Lochnagar" is from J. Scott Skinner's manuscript. Robert Burns used the melody for his poem by the same name. Its composer was Mrs. Patrick Gibson, from Edinburgh, born Isabella Mary Scott, an accomplished harpist and singer who was related to Sir Walter Scott.

In about 1924, Skinner sent a hand-written manuscript of his arrangement of "Dark Lochnagar" to his good friend, Alexander "Battan" Grant (1856–1942), who was an ardent fiddler. Skinner notes on the manuscript, "tune by Miss Gibson, 1841." He also scribbled at the bottom of the page,

> *"This melody is tears and blood."*

Tulloch Castle

D major

"A Lady" (date unknown)

This is one of the rare 19th-century strathspeys composed by a woman, whose identity, unfortunately, is known only as "a Lady." The tune appeared in William Morrison's collection, and is printed in *Highland Collections* published by the Highland Music Trust. Morrison lived from about 1780 to 1825, which places this tune most likely in the first decade of the 19th century.

The tune has a lyrical quality, made more poignant and pure by the ascent to the high D. This makes it a slight challenge for fiddle players, who will need to shift to third position to play the tune well.

The 12th-century Tulloch Castle, now a hotel, stands northwest of Inverness, in the Highlands. James Scott Skinner composed a different tune with the same name, in C minor, in 1890.

North Side of Spey

A minor

Charles Grant, 1810–1892

Charles Grant was a schoolmaster at Aberlour, and known as a fine violinist and composer. He was often called upon to be a judge at prize competitions.

The road along the north side of Spey is mentioned in a "Description of the Hills, Glens, and Passes in the Counties of Aberdeen, July 9, 1747,"* as being particularly favored by cattle thieves heading up into the mountains. The terrain on the north side of the Spey going northwest to Loch Ness is rugged and remote, difficult to traverse—even today, there are not many roads to choose from.

This strathspey is as rugged and spiky as that region; it has some teeth in it!

*From *Historical Papers Relating to the Jacobite Period, 1699–1750*, Vol. 2, ed. Col. James Allardyce, Aberdeen, 1896

Dunnotar Castle

D major

Attributed to James Young, 1815–1851

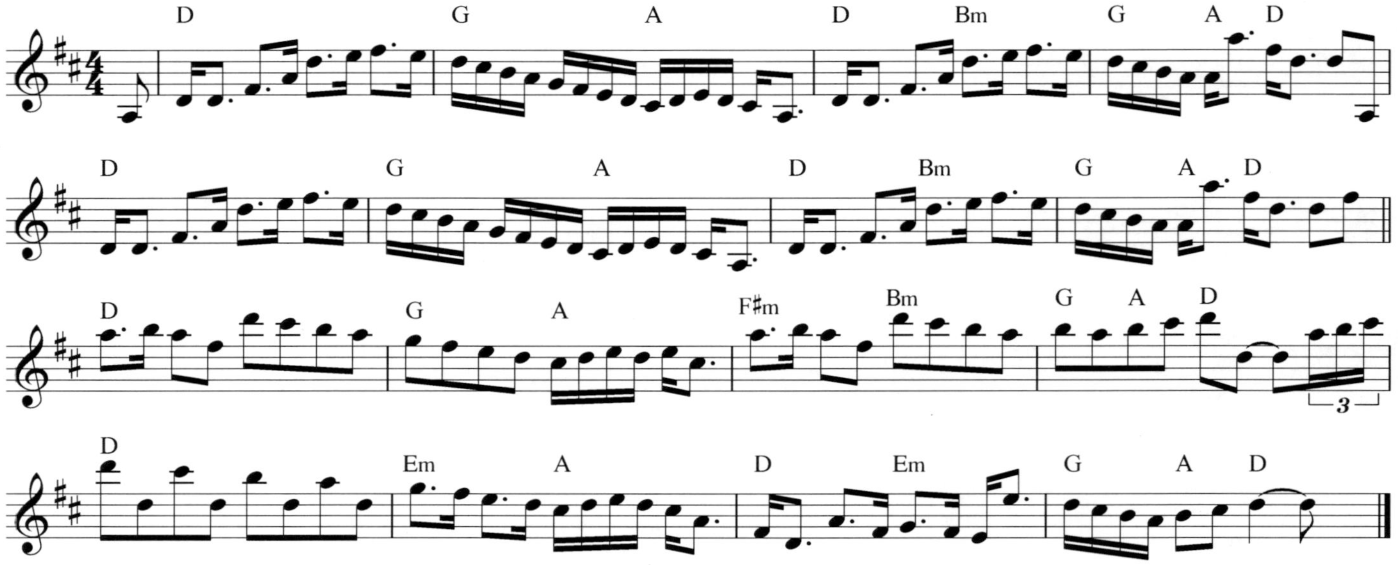

Dunnottar Castle is a commanding ruin perched on the rocky cliffs overlooking the North Sea near Stonehaven, not far from Aberdeen. Originally a Pictish fortress, later becoming a small town of turrets and towers, the castle has a dark and dramatic history. It barely survived an attack by William Wallace in 1297, who "burnt up the kirk and all that was therein"—including the soldiers and citizens who were there at the time. In 1685, during one of numerous rebellions, more than 150 men and women were held for months in a in a tiny, lightless dungeon later called the Black Hole or "Whigs' Vault." Many of them died; they are immortalized in Sir Walter Scott's novel, *Red Gauntlet*.

Dunnotar Castle, facing the North Sea

Dunnottar also housed the Scottish Regalia—the crown, sword, and sceptre—to prevent them from being taken by the English. The treasure was heroically smuggled out under the nose of Oliver Cromwell after he had lain siege to the castle for eight months.

James Young, very likely the composer of this strathspey, was a violinist, and leader of the orchestra in the Aberdeen Theatre Royal. His brother, John Young (1811–1866), was a well-respected violin-maker.

Stirling Castle

D major

Prof. Charles Bannatyne, late 19th century

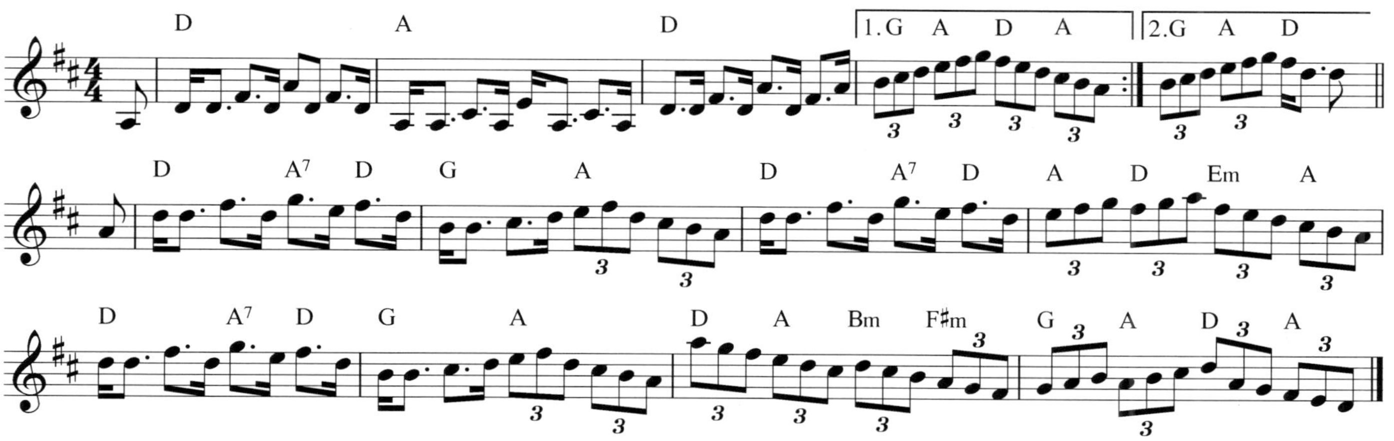

This much-loved, powerful strathspey has become an essential part of any Scottish musician's repertoire.

Stirling Castle was an ancient strategic site long before the existing castle was built in the 15th century. It was a Pictish settlement during the 9th century AD; before that the steep-cliffed hill was occupied by numerous Celtic tribes, and fortified by the Romans. Stirling was also known by a more poetic name of Snowdoun, as in Sir Walter Scott's *The Lady of the Lake* (1825):

> ...for Stirling's tower
> Of yore the name of Snowdoun claims...
> (from Canto VI of *The Lady of the Lake*)

The Castle played a starring role in the history of Scotland. It was the heart of a tug-of-war between England and Scotland, as both kingdoms wrested power and lands from each other over many centuries. The Battle of Bannockburn, in 1314, was a pivotal moment when Robert Bruce, king of the Scots, reclaimed control of the royal castle from England. In 1543, an infant Mary, Queen of Scots was crowned in Stirling Castle's Chapel Royal. Twenty-two years later, she fell in love with her second husband, Lord Darnley, as she cared for him while he recovered from measles during a stay at Stirling Castle. The castle has survived centuries of war, siege, fires, and treason; it has been the stage for murders and romance, and has hosted many royal visits.

The Stirling Jug was the official Pint measure for Scotland from the early 16th century until 1707. It is about 3.25 imperial pints.

Loch Muick

F# minor

Alexander Walker, 1819–c. 1900

Loch Muick is a small lake at the base of Lochnagar, on the Balmoral estate in Aberdeenshire. Miles of footpaths take you on a circuit around the loch, past Queen Victoria's cottage, Glas-allt-Shiel, that she built after Prince Albert's death; past waterfalls, and on to the steep ascent of Lochnagar.

Like Loch Ard, the area around Loch Muick is a haven for wildlife, especially red deer.

There was more than one Alexander Walker who was known as a fiddler during the early 19th century in Scotland. The Alexander Walker who wrote "Loch Muick" was born in Rhynie, Strathbogie, Aberdeenshire. Along with his interest in gardening and in fiddle-playing, he was a surveyor, and invented instruments for land-surveying and levelling. He became acquainted with Sir Charles Forbes of Newe in about 1851, when Walker was readying some of his newly-invented surveying instruments for the Great Exhibition. Sir Charles employed him for many years as a gardener and musician at Castle Newe.

In 1870, Walker decided to emigrate to America and join his brother in Vermont, later moving to Williamstown, Massachusetts. He continued to write tunes in the Scottish style; there are now about 200 known to be his compositions.

Towie Castle

F# minor

Alexander Walker, 1819–c. 1900

Towie Castle was a three-story fortress built about 1618 in Aberdeenshire. The towers and battlements were destroyed and dismantled in 1788; by the mid-1800s, tourist books referred to the castle as "a ruined square tower, the remnant of a stronghold of the family of Forbes." The last remains of the castle were demolished and removed in the 1980s.

Towie Castle ruins, c. 1920, from an old postcard

Like many composers, Alexander Walker wrote tunes whose titles are drawn from the area he lived in, and he lived close by Towie Castle. The ruins of Towie Castle were still standing when he lived in that area. He wrote many strathspeys besides "Towie Castle," one in honor of his employer, "Sir Charles Forbes, Baronet of Newe." Another, called "Balmoral Castle," hints at his familiarity with the royal house, as he was a member of the orchestra there.

Kildrummy Castle

B minor

Alexander Walker, 1819–c. 1900

Near the site of Towie Castle in Aberdeenshire are the dramatic ruins of Kildrummy Castle, a thirteenth-century fortress. An imposing and beautiful castle, it was considered impregnable. Edward I of England stayed as a guest at Kildrummy in 1294, and in 1303; he may have asked his stonemason to give advice on the construction of the gatehouse.

In 1306, Robert Bruce declared himself King of Scotland, and relations between Scotland and England deteriorated. To protect his wife, daughter, and sisters, Bruce had his brother, Neil, escort the ladies to Kildrummy Castle, where they would be safe. The castle was besieged and burned. Neil was executed. Robert Bruce's wife, daughter, and sisters were imprisoned. Bruce would not see his wife again until 1314, when she was released from captivity. In the meantime, he set upon a path of relentless struggle against Edward and the English monarchy.

Kildrummy Castle was repeatedly repaired and besieged in the next 500 years, a dramatic venue for the ceaseless battle between Scotland and the Crown of England.

Statue of Robert Bruce at Stirling Castle

Devil in the Kitchen

A mixolydian

William Ross (Queen's Piper), 1823–1891

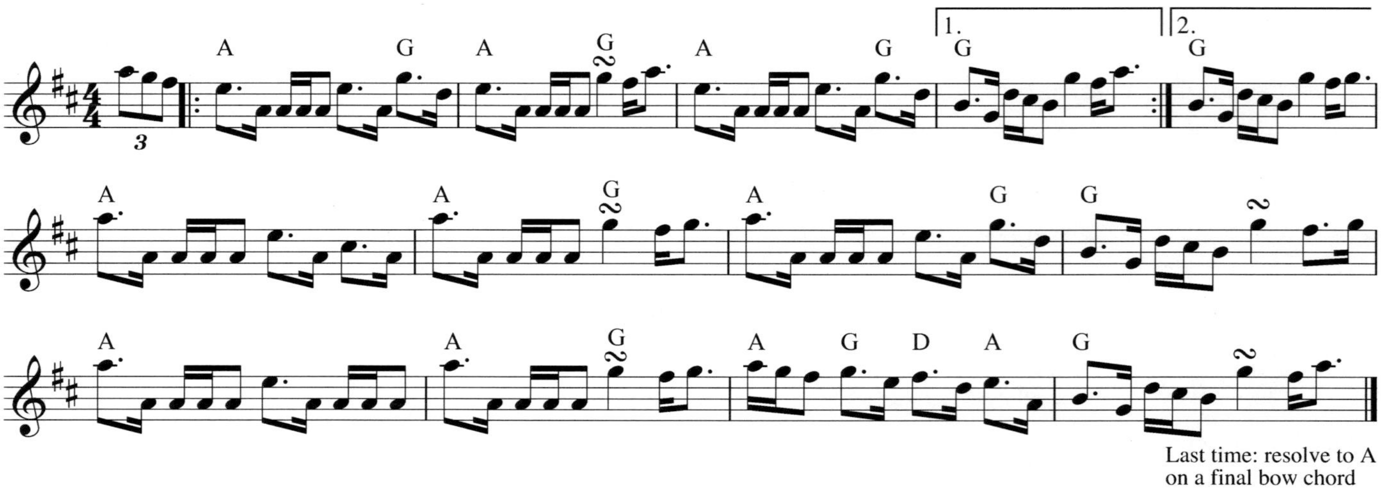

This pipe strathspey is a classic—energetic, spiky, full of spunk. James Scott Skinner published it in his *Harp and Claymore* collection (1903), noting that it should be played an octave lower the second time through the tune. As you might expect from a tune written for bagpipe, it welcomes embellishments and ornamentation. The key of A mixolydian is the key of A major, without the G sharp.

The term "devil" often is used for the youngest apprentice in a shop or business establishment. A "printer's devil" is an apprentice who helps out in the print shop; in a big kitchen, the "devil" would probably tend the fire and turn the spits.

Aboyne Castle
(The Marchioness of Huntly)

A major

Peter Milne, 1824–1908

A strong strathspey, in the triumphant key of A major!

Peter Milne was born in Kincardine O'Neil, near Banchory and Aboyne. The 15th-century castle at Aboyne was part of the holdings of the Gordons, the Marquis of Huntly, in the "Royal Deeside" area of Aberdeenshire.

Milne taught himself to play the fiddle when he was in his teens, and quickly became very good at it. By the time he was in his twenties, he was heading up a band and playing at the Theatre Royal in Aberdeen. He became friends with J. Scott Skinner, and ended up hiring him, not as a fiddle player, but as a cellist, to play with his band. He eventually moved to Edinburgh, playing at several theaters there, and went on to tour England for a while. After spending some time in England, Milne returned to Scotland, earning part of his living as a fiddler entertaining the ferry passengers as they crossed the Firth of Forth. When the new Forth Road took the place of the ferries, and put him out of a job, Milne returned to Aberdeen, where he continued to play in theaters, played for dances, and also taught violin. It was probably a tenuous existence.

Milne may have written many tunes; unfortunately, they were not published in a collection, and only a few are known to be his compositions. Skinner acknowledged him as a fine musician, publishing one of his tunes in his *Harp and Claymore* collection, with the following note: "Peter Milne was the founder of the present style of Strathspey playing, and the best all round player and composer of his day. His left hand was as unerring and accurate as a machine."

Forbes Morrison

A major

J. Scott Skinner, 1843–1927

In 1863, J. Scott Skinner entered a strathspey competition in Inverness. He won it, but the runner-up was evidently worth remembering, as Skinner wrote this strathspey dedicated to him, Mr. Forbes Morrison. Mr. Morrison (1833–1906) was a dancing-master who lived in Tarves, Aberdeenshire.

You can listen to a recording of Skinner playing this tune, with many variations, at the University of Aberdeen website (http://www.abdn.ac.uk/scottskinner/discography.shtml), where many of his recordings and original manuscripts have been archived.

Dancing-masters used a small fiddle, called a pochette, or a kit, small enough to tuck away while teaching a dance.

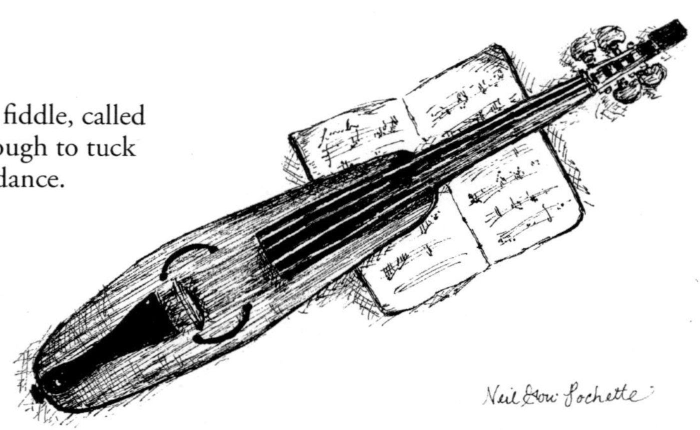

John McNiell's Highland Fling

A mixolydian

J. Scott Skinner, 1843–1927

An energetic, A-mixolydian tune, this tune is a bagpipe strathspey. All Gs are closer to being natural, not sharped, on the bagpipes; fiddlers can often choose whether or not to make them G sharp or G natural. In this case, however, Skinner has notated the Gs to be played as naturals.

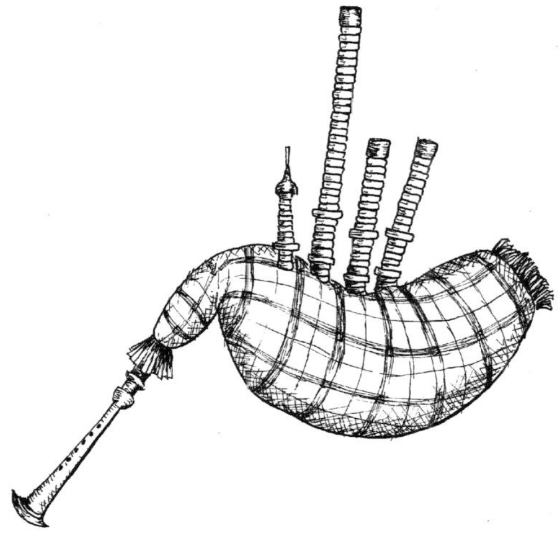

The Kirrie Kebbuck

D major

James Scott Skinner, 1843–1927

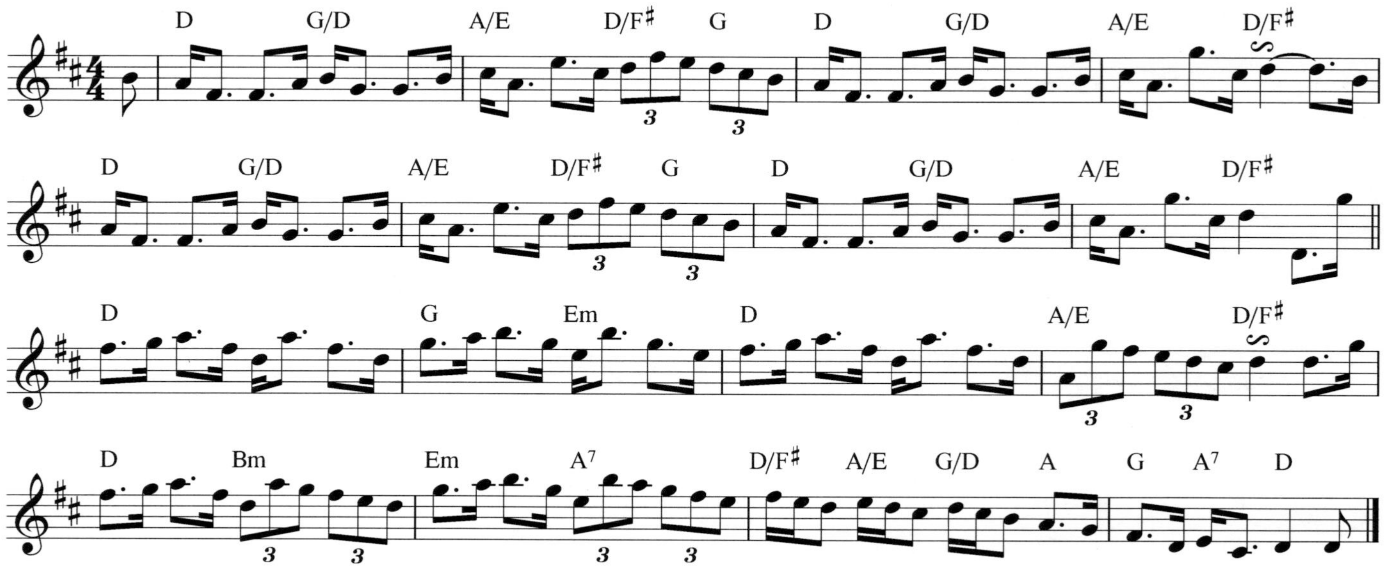

“Kebbuck” is the Scots term for a large, whole wheel of cheese. J. Scott Skinner dedicated this tune in 1908 to his friend, Alex McPherson, with the following inscription on the manuscript page: “To A McPherson, the Laird o’ Thrums....” When McPherson’s tenants came to pay him their rent, he would always offer them a drop of whisky, some bread, and a slice of “kebbuck.” Skinner notes at the bottom of the manuscript page, “The Kirrie Kebbuck...an amazing operation upon a huge Cheese performed by ‘The Laird’ wi’ a saw!” It might just be possible to hear the Laird sawing off a piece of cheese as you listen to the rhythm of the music...

Kirrie is the town of Kirriemuir, made famous as the town of “Thrums” in J. M. Barrie’s book, *A Window in Thrums*. Barrie was better-known as the creator of Peter Pan, and a statue of Peter Pan stands in the town of Kirriemuir, where Barrie lived.

Mr. A .G. Wilken's Favourite

F major

J. Scott Skinner, 1843–1927

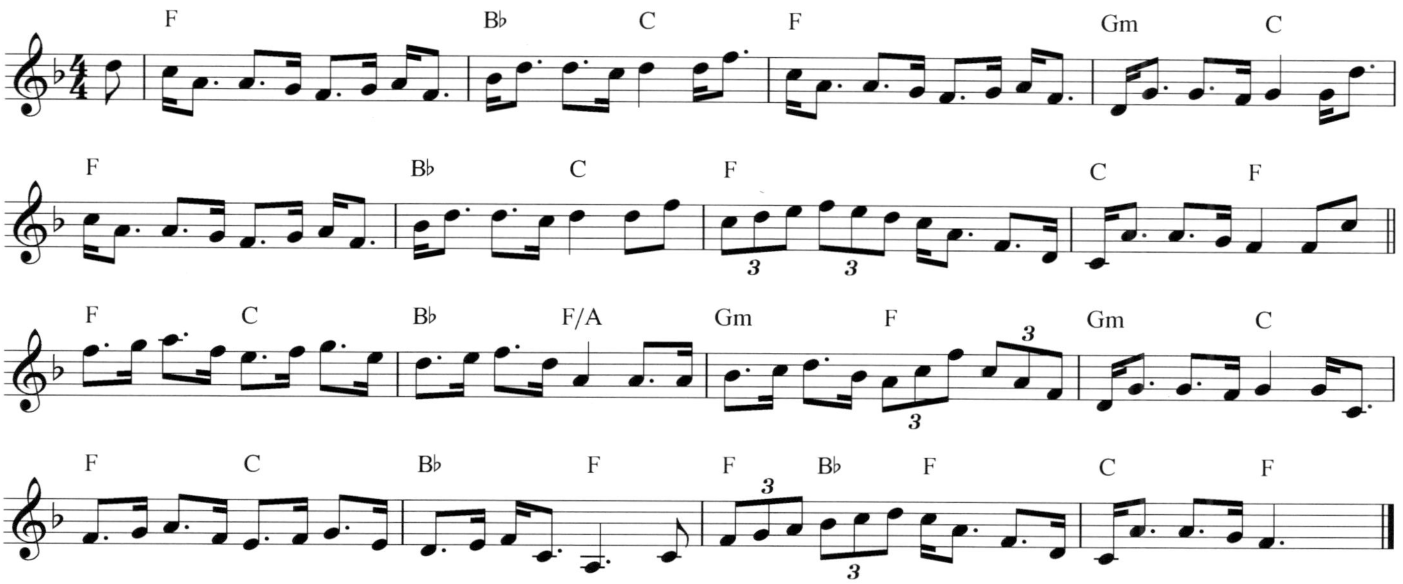

James Scott Skinner, the self-styled "Strathspey King," composed volumes of tunes, and published several collections of tunes by others. His first major collection was *The Miller o' Hirn Collection*, in 1881, and it contained 122 tunes (strathspeys, reels, Highland schottisches, airs, songs, jigs, and hornpipes) arranged for violin and pianoforte or cello. Some of the tunes are named after fiddlers, and this is one of them. Mr. A. G. Wilken was an amateur violinist from the village of Ellon, Aberdeenshire.

The Music o' Spey

A major

J. Scott Skinner, 1843–1927

J. Scott Skinner composed this lovely strathspey and published it in his *Miller o' Hirn* collection in 1881.

This is a pastoral strathspey, as opposed to the strong kind of strathspeys that tend to be angular and full of bite. Pastoral strathspeys are smoother, less replete with snaps, and they usually sound as if they might have lyrics (many of them do).

There is some gray area about whether pastoral strathspeys are the same as song strathspeys. In general, whatever you call them (pastoral or song), these strathspeys have few snaps, and they have a smooth, flowing motion.

The words to "The Music o' Spey," which were printed in Skinner's *Miller o' Hirn* collection, were written by R. Grant, from Peterhead, Aberdeenshire. The River Ugie runs through that region; Grant was known as "the Bard of Ugie."

Lyrics to "The Music o' Spey"
by R. Grant

I sing o' the Spey, the bonnie, bonnie Spey,
Whar the primrose grows so early,
An' ilka mile o' the bonnie Hielan' stream
Can shew you some rare fairlie.

Oh dearly I lo'e the grand auld Spey,
And its music aye sae cheerie,
Whan I hear the soun' o' my ain dear stream ;
I ne'er feel dow nor weary.
. . .

There's Naething Like the "Talisker"

A mixolydian

J. Scott Skinner, 1843–1927

Skinner wrote this tune in honor of Roderick Kemp, part owner of the Talisker whisky distillery on the Isle of Skye. Kemp was also a judge at the Inverness competition of 1863, where Skinner won first prize for his fiddle playing.

The original manuscript in the University of Aberdeen is written in Skinner's strong handwriting, and the title, as he wrote it, is "Ters naesing like ta 'Talisker'" with his dedication to R. Kemp beneath.

Tillydaff

G minor

By "A Lady," 2011

A good amount of the background information and ideas for the illustrations in this book came from two trips to Scotland to visit friends who own a beautiful organic farm—North Tillydaff, Aberdeenshire. Farming is tough work, unpredictable, full of grit and aches and getting dirt under one's nails. But the beauty of the landscape, with the mist-covered summit of Bennachie in the distance, makes it feel a noble way of life.   I wrote this tune for Anne and Wendy, in thanks for wonderful times at North Tillydaff.

Sources and References

Alburger, Mary Anne. *Scottish Fiddlers and Their Music.* Edinburgh, The Hardie Press, 1996. A valuable source of historical information about the Scottish fiddle tradition.

Banner, Jane M. *Braes o' Tullymet.* Perth & Kinross District Libraries, 1988. Detailed information about the region around Tullymet.

Baptie, David. *Musical Scotland, Past and Present, Being a Dictionary of Scottish Musicians from About 1400 to the Present Time.* Paisley, Scotland, J. and R. Parlane, 1894.

Black, Adam and Charles. *Black's Picturesque Tourist of Scotland* (18th ed.). Edinburgh, 1869.

Boswell, James. *The Journal of a Tour to the Hebrides with Samuel Johnson.* First published 1785. Available through Project Gutenberg (www.gutenberg.org).

Bremner, Robert. *A Collection of Scots Reels or Country Dances.* London, c. 1765.

Carlin, Richard, compiler and editor. *The Gow Collection of Scottish Dance Music.* New York, Oak Publications, 1986. Good introductory material about the Gows.

Collins Pocket Scots Dictionary, the essential guide to modern Scots. Glasgow, HarperCollins,1996.

Cowie, Moyra. *The Life and Times of William Marshall.* Elgin, Scotland, 1999.

Cranford, Paul Stewart, compiler and editor. *Alexander Walker Collection of Fiddle Tunes.* Cape Breton Island, Cranford Publications, 1997. Good information about Alexander Walker's life; tunes arranged by key.

Cumming, Angus. *A Collection of Strathspeys or old Highland Reels.* Edinburgh, 1780.

Emmerson, George S. *Rantin' Pipe and Tremblin' String: history of Scottish dance music.* London, Canada, 1988.

Findlay, H. L. *A Book of Scotland.* London and Glasgow [n.d.]. Poems, quotations, essays.

Fraser, Capt. Simon. *Airs and Melodies Peculiar to the Highlands and Isles of Scotland.* Edinburgh and London, 1816. Reprinted by Paul Stewart Cranford, Cape Breton Island, 1982. Fraser includes some explanatory notes about many of the tunes in the collection.

French, John. *A Collection of New Strathspey Reels.* Edinburgh, c. 1801. A collection of Scots tunes available in PDF format from the The Highland Music Trust website, www.heallan.com.

Glen, John. *Glen Collection of Scottish Dance Music.* Edinburgh, 2 volumes, 1891, 1895. Glen has extensive biographical notes at the beginning of each volume.

Hardie, Alastair J. *The Caledonian Companion.* Edinburgh, The Hardie Press, 1992.

Highland Music Trust. *Highland Collections: The Music of Seven 18th and 19th Century Fiddler-Composers from the Highlands of Scotland (William Christie, Isaac Cooper, Angus Cumming, Charles Grant, Donald Grant, James Henry, William Morrison).* Inverness, Highland Music Trust, 2005.

Hogg, James. *Songs, by the Ettrick Shepherd.* Edinburgh, William Blackwood, 1831.

Honeyman, William C. *The Strathspey, Reel, and Hornpipe Tutor.* 1898.

— "Strathspey Players Past and Present." Edinburgh, Larg & Sons, 1922. Reprinted by Ogmios Press, 2002.

Hunter, James. *The Fiddle Music of Scotland.* Edinburgh, 1979. Very helpful background information in the introduction, and some notes about individual tunes in an appendix.

Johnson, David. *Scottish Fiddle Music in the 18th Century, a music collection and historical study.* 3rd edition. Edinburgh, 2005.

Johnson, James. *The Scots Musical Museum.* 6 volumes. Edinburgh, 1787–1803.

Kuntz, Andrew. "The King of the Patrons," *Fiddler Magazine*, Summer 2005.

Lowe, Joseph. *Lowe's Collection of Reels, Strathspeys, and Jigs, Being a New and Complete Selection of the Best Dancing Tunes in Their Proper Keys.* Books 1–6. Edinburgh, Paterson & Sons, c. 1844.

Mac(k)intosh, Robert. *Airs, Minuets, Gavotts and Reels.* Edinburgh, 1783.

Mackintosh, Robert. *Sixty-eight New Reels, Strathspeys, and Quicksteps.* 4 volumes. Edinburgh, 1792, 1793, 1794; London, 1804.

Martin, Christine, compiler. *Traditional Scottish Fiddling, A Player's Guide to Regional Styles, Bowing Techniques, Repertoire and Dances.* Isle of Skye, Scotland, Taigh na Teud, 2002. Contains an excellent introduction to Scottish regional styles, bowing techniques, and ornamentation.

Maxwell, Sir Michael. "Lady Jane Maxwell," a speech to the Clan Maxwell Society of the USA, 1997.

Miller, Randy, editor. *William Marshall's Scottish Melodies: 262 Strathspeys, Reels, Hornpipes, Marches, Jigs & Airs.* 2nd ed. Fiddlecase Books, 2007. A collection of Marshall's works compiled from six volumes originally published in Edinburgh between 1781 and 1845.

MacDonald, Keith Norman, editor. *The Skye Collection of the Best Reels & Strathspeys Extant, Embracing over four hundred tunes.* Originally published 1887. Reprinted by Paul Stewart Cranford, Cape Breton Island, in 1979.

— *The Gesto Collection of Highland Music,* compiled and arranged by Keith Norman MacDonald (1895). Reprinted by Llanerch Publishers, Ceredigion, Wales, 1997.

McDonald, Patrick. *A Collection of Highland Vocal Airs, never hitherto published, to which are added a few of the most lively Country Dances or Reels of the North Highlands and Western Isles.* Edinburgh, 1784.

Morison, Jane Fraser. *Highland Airs & Quicksteps.* Inverness, Logan & Co., 1882. A collection of Scots tunes available in PDF format from the The Highland Music Trust website, www.heallan.com.

Neil, J. Murray. *The Scots Fiddle (Vol. 1): Tunes, Tales & Traditions of the North-East and Central Highlands.* Glasgow, 1999.

Oswald, James. *A curious collection of Scots tunes.* Edinburgh, 1739.

— *The Caledonian Pocket Companion.* 15 volumes. London, c. 1747–1769.

Petrie, Robert. *A Collection of Strathspey Reels & Country Dances.* 3 volumes. Edinburgh, 1795–1800. A collection of Scots tunes available in PDF format from the The Highland Music Trust website, www.heallan.com.

Pringle, John. *A Collection of Reels, Strathspeys & Jigs.* Edinburgh, 1801. A collection of Scots tunes available in PDF format from the The Highland Music Trust website, www.heallan.com.

Robertson, James Stewart, compiler and editor. *The Athole Collection of the Dance Music of Scotland.* Originally published in 1884; reprinted by Balnain House Trust, Inverness, 1996.

Shepherd, William. *A Collection of Strathspey Reels.* Edinburgh, c. 1793. An early collection of Scots tunes available in PDF format from the The Highland Music Trust website, www.heallan.com.

Sim, Alan. "200 Years of Making North-east Fiddles," *Leopard: The Magazine for North-East Scotland.* June 2005. Interesting information about Peter Hardie, Peter Milne, Niel Gow, and the tradition of fiddle-making in Scotland in the 18th and 19th centuries.

Skinner, J. Scott. *The Harp and Claymore, a Volume of Music,* ed. Gavin Grieg, 1904. Introduction to the collection is by Skinner, entitled "The Strathspey."

Surenne, John Thomas. *The Dance Music of Scotland.* Edinburgh, 1851. A collection of Scots tunes available in PDF format from the The Highland Music Trust website, www.heallan.com.

Welsh, Mary, and Isherwood, Christine. *Walking Strathspey: Moray, Banff and Buchan.* Doune, Perthshire, Clan Walk Guides, 2009.

Suggestions for Tune Medleys

Creating a medley of tunes is a bit of an adventure. Factors to think about would be the personality of each tune, the key it's written in, and beginning and ending melody notes. Moving from one tune to another is probably the hardest thing about creating a medley—tune transitions can make or break it.

Because I know there may be some people looking at this book with an eye to using the tunes for Scottish country dances as well as for concerts and solo performances, here is a brief list of some possible sets of tunes that might be suitable for country dances. *Large disclaimer here:* please take this list with a chunk of salt! This is meant to be a guide, not a prescribed list writ in stone. Your results may vary....chords may be changed, playing styles may differ, the range of the instrument played may dictate either a slight re-write or a transposition of the tune. When creating medleys, your ear is your best guide. Watch the dancers—their movements will help you shape the tune to the dance.

Brief note about dances and title tunes: Some of these tunes are also considered title tunes, or "signature tunes" associated with a certain dance. They would be the first tune in a medley for that dance. For example, "The Music of Spey" is the title tune for the dance called *Miss Gibson's Strathspey.* It's probably all right if you use it as the second or third tune in a medley for a different dance, but avoid using it as the first tune for the dance called *Birks of Invermay,* which uses the tune called "Birks of Invermay." If you are playing for a Scottish country dance, and you are not sure about tunes, check with the dance organizers to make sure you are using the correct title tune for each dance, and ask for some guidance from a musician who has played for Scottish country dances before. There is also a very useful website, "the Strathspey Server," at http://my.strathspey.org/dd/index.html, that provides a dance database by dance title, tune title, recording, publication, and other key information.

Pastoral and Song Strathspeys	Pipe Strathspeys
The Mill Mill O (D)	John McNiell's (A modal)
Birks of Invermay (G)	The Haughs of Cromdale (Am)
O Were I On Parnassus Hill (Em)	Devil in the Kitchen (A modal)
	Cutting Ferns (Am)
Mary Morrison (F)	
The Music of Spey (A)	
The Banks of Spey (Am)	

Strong / Lyrical Strathspeys	
Lady Brome's (Cm)	South of the Grampians (A)
Croughly (Dm)	Panmure House / Miss Lyall (Am)
Bridge of Brechin (F)	Stirling Castle (D)
Queen's Landing (Bm)	Ruffian's Rant (D)
Miss Jessie Smith (D)	Rothemurches Rant (C)
Mrs. McInroy of Lude (Bm)	Rob Roy MacGregor (Em) (don't repeat A part)
Mrs. James Duff's (A)	